Honoring Our Ancestral Obligations

1

As a bonus resource, this book contains a QR code that you can scan (below) using your phone to gain free access to 15 brief video clips about key concepts in this book.

Praise for Honoring Our Ancestral Obligations

XIIIIXIIIIXIIIIXIIIIX CHIKE AKUA XIIIIXIIIIXIIIIXIIIIX

Honoring Our Ancestral Obligations

"*Every life is precious and every body is a sacred vessel which ancestors inhabit to order continue their soul's work. When we understand the value of* Honoring Our Ancestral Obligations, *we make it possible for our ancestors to awaken the genius within us so that we fulfill our reason for living.*

<u>With his publication, **Honoring Our Ancestral Obligations, Dr. Akua has provided students with the tools to make positive choices in their academic and personal lives.**</u> *Such guidance is the real purpose of an education which will benefit humanity for many generations.*

As an educator, Dr. Chike Akua has learned from the best. He is fulfilling his Ancestral Obligations and continues to make those who educated extremely proud."

    Anthony T. Browder, Director & Author
    IKG and the ASA Restoration Project
    Nile Valley Contributions to Civilizations

"*In this volume (and in all of his chosen work),* <u>**Dr. Chike Akua provides an impressive, readable, yet comprehensive guide to assisting in the work of path finding for our youth.**</u> *He honors his Ancestral Obligations and all of us by 're-minding,' 're-membering,' and 're-presenting' our youth to their ancestral origins, brand and responsibility."*

    Na'im Akbar, Ph.D., Clinical Psychologist & Author
    Breaking the Chains of Psychological Slavery; Know Thyself
    New Visions for Black Men; Light From Ancient Africa

"Dr. Chike Akua provides powerful insight into why and how students and adults can experience greater power through honoring the ancestral voice within that calls us all to live beyond mediocrity and to manifest greatness. **'Honoring Our Ancestral Obligations' is a powerful read for the elevation of consciousness and healing of the soul.** Dr. Akua reminds students that excellence is a part of their biogenetic make up."

    Dr. Kevin Washington, Psychologist
    Professor, Howard University
    President, The Association of Black Psychologists

Honoring Our Ancestral Obligations

"My team and I started a new Servant Leadership Academy for African American High School students and wanted to infuse the lessons with cultural components that we knew were important for our students to learn. <u>After reading Dr. Chike Akua's book, Honoring Our Ancestral Obligations, I knew immediately how to apply our vision and purpose for the academy. This book is perfect for both students and adults to follow and immediately apply to learning practices</u> and it shows clearly the power and beauty of our people in a way that made our young people proud of their heritage and also challenged them to change the way they think about themselves. Each chapter could be applied to life both in the community and at school and each month our students grew into more socially and culturally confident young people that we are proud to say are "Honoring Our Ancestral Obligations". Thank you, Dr. Akua, for this precious tool and resource."

       Angelia Barfield, Ed.D.
       Coordinator II, Student Intervention & Prevention
       Fresno County Office of Education
       Fresno, CA

<u>"Students today find themselves in learning environments of cultural isolation. They are thirsty for knowledge and understanding</u> from having to navigate the seemly abyss of negativity they find themselves in. Dr. Chike Akua's "Honoring Our Ancestral Obligations" provides a light house, a north star for them to follow!"
       Mr. Fluke Fluker, Award-Winning Educator
       Founder of The Village Nation
       Los Angeles, CA

"No matter their circumstances or knowledge base, this book is a gift to young minds with the capacity to see and be Afrikan. <u>It is full of the vision, possibilities, methods and lessons we need for ourselves and our children to so easily become sovereign.</u> Meda ase pii (thank you) for this centered educational effort. Abibifahodie (Afrikan liberation)."
       Mwalimu K. Bomani Baruti, Author
       Asafo: A Warrior's Guide to Manhood
       IWA: A Warrior's Character

Honoring
Our Ancestral Obligations
7 Steps To Black Student Success
By
Chike Akua, Ph.D.

Published by
Imani Enterprises
Fourth Edition ©2022 Chike Akua
Third Edition ©2021 Chike Akua
Second Edition ©2017 Chike Akua
First Edition ©2015 Chike Akua
All Rights Reserved
ISBN: 978-0-9704644-2-2

www.DrAkua.net

Other Books By Dr. Chike Akua

Education for Transformation: The Keys to Releasing the Genius of African American Students (10 Year Anniversary 2ND Edition) (2022)

Words of Power, Volume 2:
Centering Ourselves for Excellence
(2020)

SuccessQuest: The Journey From Ordinary to Extraordinary
(2017)

ParentPower:
The Keys to Your Child's Academic & Social Success
(2012)

Sexceptional:
The Ultimate & Essential Teen Guide to Abstinence
(2012)

Reading Revolution: Reconnecting the Roots
(with Tavares Stephens)
(2006)

Words of Power, Volume 1: Ancient Insights & Modern Messages for Parents, Teachers, and Students (2005)

A Kwanzaa Awakening: Lessons for the Community
(4th Edition) (2004)

The African Origins of Our Faith (2004)

A Treasure Within: Stories of Remembrance & Rediscovery (2001)

A Treasure Within: Parent/Teacher Resource Guide (2001)

Honoring Our Ancestral Obligations

6
Special Thanks

To my wife of over 28 years, Willette, my partner in love, life and liberation, for continuing love and support

To my sons, Jahbari and Amari, for inspiring me to strive to be a great father

To my parents, Joseph and Faye Fenwick, for the example of loving, supportive and visionary parents with strong values

To my sister, Leslie Fenwick, and my brothers, Russell, John and Jason: lights and guides in times of trial, tribulation, triumph and victory

To Dr. Damira Shields, for editorial assistance

To Nana Kra Kwamina & Nana Obokese for visionary leadership

To Baba Ali & Mama Helen Salahuddin, for guidance and continuous opportunities to share my gifts and purpose

To Dr. Joyce King, for intellectual inspiration and cultural centering

To my friend and brother, Jahi Chikwendu Muhammad and Mama Kyna Clemons for editorial assistance

To Delxino & Debbie Wilson de Briano, for continuing the work of the Honorable Marcus Garvey through www.BuyBlackMovement.com

To Baba Wekesa & Mama Afiya Madzimoyo, for self-determination

To The Knowledge Keepers:
George Fraser, Tony Browder, Nana Kwa David Whittaker & Bob Lott, for vision, strength and unity

To Baba Mwalimu Bomani Baruti & Mama Yaa Baruti, for a continuing example of centered steadfastness and dedication

To Dr. Stephen Tates for guidance in health and wellness.

To Mama Marie West & Mama Rosalyn Martin, for the covering of prayer

Dedication

For Nana Baffour Amakwatia II (Dr. Asa G. Hilliard III)
We will continue what you have begun.

XIIIIXIIIIXIIIIXIIIIX **CHIKE AKUA** XIIIIXIIIIXIIIIXIIIIX

Honoring Our Ancestral Obligations

*****To the Reader**

It is not by chance that this book has come into your possession. What you are about to read will transform your life in every way. Read and be wise, then share it with a friend.

*A scroll is a symbol of ancient wisdom. In ancient times, African scribes would write their scientific discoveries and deep knowledge on papyrus scrolls. These scrolls contained the wisdom of the ages and many still exist today. Also in ancient times, the symbol of the Udjat (First Eye) represented deep insight. Every time you see a scroll and Udjat in this book, it contains deep wisdom and insight for you to pause and think about.

XIIIIXIIIIXIIIIXIIIIX   CHIKE AKUA   XIIIIXIIIIXIIIIXIIIIX

Table of Contents

9	Forward By Professor Kaba Kamene
10	Preface by Dr. Arnett Mpigani Kweli
12	Introduction To Your Higher Self
20	About the Cover
23	Step 1: Identity Restoration
27	Centering Ourselves for the Journey Ahead
31	Authentic v. Alien Cultural Images
33	Critical Thinking to Reclaim Consciousness
43	Step 2: Education for Liberation
57	The Past, Power & Potential of HBCUs
60	Keys to Unlocking Cultural Memory
63	Step 3: Economic Mobilization
68	The Solution
74	Learning & Practicing the Skill of Investing
76	Power & Political Participation
79	Step 4: Calling & Career Preparation
90	Countering Mass Incarceration
101	Step 5: Spiritual Transformation
106	Seven Observations About Spirit
109	Seven Principles of Kwanzaa
112	Seven Ways to Cultivate Spiritual Power
115	Step 6: Relationship Revolution & Family Restoration
121	Cultivating Healthy Relationships
129	Step 7: Health & Wellness Resuscitation
139	Mastering Our Mental Health
153	Mastering Our Melanin
160	Afterword: Walking into Our Destiny…
165	The Ancestral Obligation Oath
167	References
172	About the Author
173	Other Books & Posters By Dr. Chike Akua

Honoring Our Ancestral Obligations

Foreword

Dr. Chike Akua's *Honoring our Ancestral Obligations*, is a timely read for every student and person of African ascent. Dr. Akua has continued the great educational legacy of Africans at home and abroad. His "7 Steps to Black Student Success," is fundamental to the learning process. It gives the reader a sense of "Self-Concept." The literary structure of *Ancestral Obligations*, is intellectually relevant. "How" you teach is as important as "What" you teach. There is a West African proverb that states, "When you have learned your lesson, you can discard it, because it was How you learned your lesson that was the true goal."

Brother Akua has developed a significant road to developing a strong and viable sense of a student's "Self Concept," in the 7 Steps he outlines for us. For example, in the beginning of the book, he explains what a scroll represents. Throughout the book, he presents thoughts, ideas and concepts written in the scrolls. Following each scroll is a learning objective that demonstrates the meaning of the scrolls. The educational process is actively applied, not just superficially learned or memorized. This "applied learning" demonstrates what ancient Kemites (Egyptians) meant when they called their schools, "Per Ankhs." *Per Ankh* means "Temple of Life."

To Africans in Kemet, learning is living and living is learning. Infusing, Ancestral Obligations into a student's life can invigorate, energize and enliven the educational process. When you know the past, you can interpret the present and project your future. The Seven Steps will take the reader/learner back to find his/her future. I strongly recommend Dr. Chike Akua's book, *Honoring Our Ancestral Obligations: 7 Steps To Black Student Success*. Sankofa…Let's return and retrieve it.

Kaba Hiawatha Kamene, Professor of Black Studies
Educator, Curriculum Writer
State University of New York, New Paltz

Honoring Our Ancestral Obligations

Preface

Dr. Chike Akua's ability to detail factual information shows him to be a topnotch scholar. His ability to communicate in an easygoing, plain-spoken manner distinguishes him as a man of the community. This book has become an essential text in my programs for teens. From thoughtful silences to full-throated passionate debate, teens respond powerfully to Dr. Akua's prose. This level of engagement is distinctive with Dr. Akua's work.

I have over 40-plus years of community education activism and 32 years as a professional educator. *I have noticed increasingly that students are less impressed by cursory knowledge about African firsts – first civilization, first to develop science, medicine, etc. They question how this knowledge makes a difference in their real lives.* The want to know what is relevant about an ancient past that can seem so ... ancient. Dr. Akua's method of contemporary discussion buttressed by references to Maatian philosophy, Yoruba spirituality, Kemetian and African diasporan history grounds the present in our ancient and recent past. Students discover a new criterion for assessing their contemporary circumstance. I have seen them excited by their own new understandings and ideas.

Most of all I appreciate how Dr. Akua's work eases the task of identity formation in young people. Popular media, especially social media, has confused our identity. Through *Honoring our Ancestral Obligations,* students connect easily with their ancestral lineage knowing it takes them to a place of intellectual riches and emotional resilience. They begin to discern presentations that are Black on the surface yet have no connection to their own culture and history. They begin to speak affirmatively of others with whom they are connected. They begin to see a future that is theirs for the making. Asante sana (thank you), Dr. Akua, they help me to see it, too.

Dr. Arnett Carl Duncan / Dr. Arnett Mpigani Kweli
Executive Director, Kweli Educational Enterprises
"Kweli means truth"

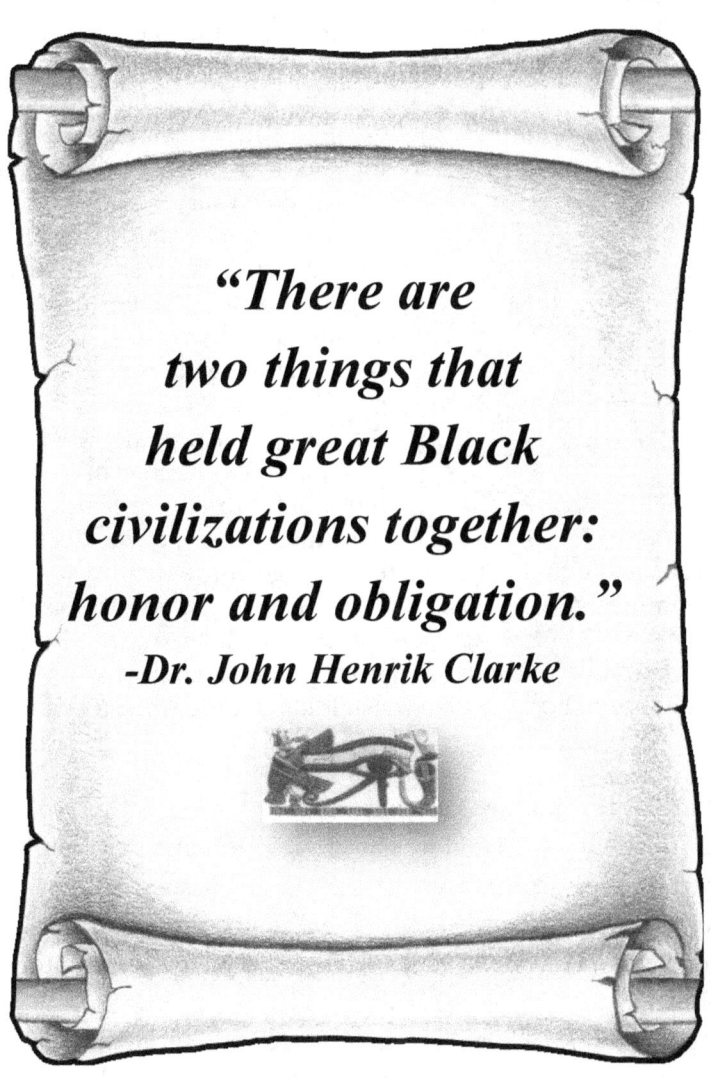

"There are two things that held great Black civilizations together: honor and obligation."
-Dr. John Henrik Clarke

Introduction to Your Higher Self

This is a book that is long overdue and the title was very carefully chosen. Dr. John Henrik Clarke, one of our most highly respected and highly regarded scholars, remarked that great African Empires, nations and civilizations were held together by two things: "honor and obligation" (Clarke, 1992).

To honor is to show deep respect. An obligation is a responsibility one has that must be fulfilled without question. So, to honor our Ancestral obligations, we must first know what an Ancestor is. An Ancestor, in African tradition and culture, is not just someone who lived long ago in your family line. An Ancestor is one who lived their life as an example of character, courage, unwavering commitment, dignity and integrity that we can take lessons from. The word Ancestor is not a proper noun that requires capitalization. I choose to make a proper noun here and capitalize it, because, in African tradition, the Ancestors are just that important.

Aso-Dsi (pronounced ah-zote-zee)

In America, we are told we have rights. But in many traditional African societies and civilizations, the emphasis was not on rights but on *responsibilities*. The Akan people of Ghana have a concept called *aso-dsi* which refers to duties, responsibilities and obligations. Prior to our enslavement, our *aso-dsi* (duties, responsibilities and obligations) were communicated through our education, socialization and rituals (Nketsia, 2013). Even during and after our enslavement there was a community consciousness that kept our *aso-dsi* alive. But now, in the absence of our authentic culture, many people are unaware and ill-equipped to

Honoring Our Ancestral Obligations

fulfill their *aso-dsi*.

So, *"Honoring Our Ancestral Obligations"* means that we will show deep respect to our Ancestors by the way we live our lives and that we will fulfill our responsibilities with character, consciousness and commitment. This is necessary for two reasons—one, it is the Divine Ancestral standard of excellence and—two, there has been a methodical erosion and virtual erasure of some of our most cherished values. When these values were violated, there used to be a sense of shame. *But there can be no shame and is no shame when the original values are not known.* This is why **there is an African Proverb which says, "Where there is no shame, there is no honor."** Take a look at videos and memes circulating on social media and some of the most popular TV shows and you will see that our sense of shame and honor has eroded tremendously.

There is an African Proverb which says, "Abundance of lies has made truth a high-priced commodity." As I have traveled around the country speaking to tens of thousands of students, teachers, business leaders, parents and professors in K-12 schools, colleges, universities, faith-based organizations, community centers and conferences, I have found that students have a *serious* thirst for the knowledge that is contained in this book. I have found this to be true, especially among students who come from the most challenging circumstances and those who do not make top grades in school. So this book contains a great deal of powerful information that is often *not* in the curriculum in most schools.

This book harmonizes with my book for teachers entitled, *Education for Transformation: The Keys to Releasing the Genius of African American Students* and my book for parents entitled, *ParentPower: The Keys to Your Child's Academic and Social Success*.

To get the most out of this book, it will be helpful to understand what culture is:

> …many students of liberation struggles have noted that culture is a weapon in a people's struggle because the suppression or denial of their culture is part of their enslavement" (Nobles, 2006, p. 196).

Wade Nobles gives a number of helpful explanations to illuminate what culture is and why it is so important:

> Culture is the vast structure of behaviors, ideas, attitudes, values, habits, beliefs, customs, language, rituals, ceremonies and practices peculiar to a particular group of people.
> - *Culture provides…a general design for living and patterns for interpreting reality.*
> - *Culture gives meaning to reality*
> - *Culture has the power to compel behavior.*
> - Culture is the invisible medium in which all human functioning occurs. It is, in fact, important to note that nothing human happens outside of culture.
> - *Culture is like the electricity that illuminates the light bulb.*
> - *Culture is to humans as water is to fish* (Nobles 2006, p. 164).

Far too often, the worst of our behavior is placed in broad media circulation and then labeled "Black culture." There is an African proverb which says, "He who does not know the real design will turn to an imitation" (Willis, 1998, p. 150). If you don't know your culture,

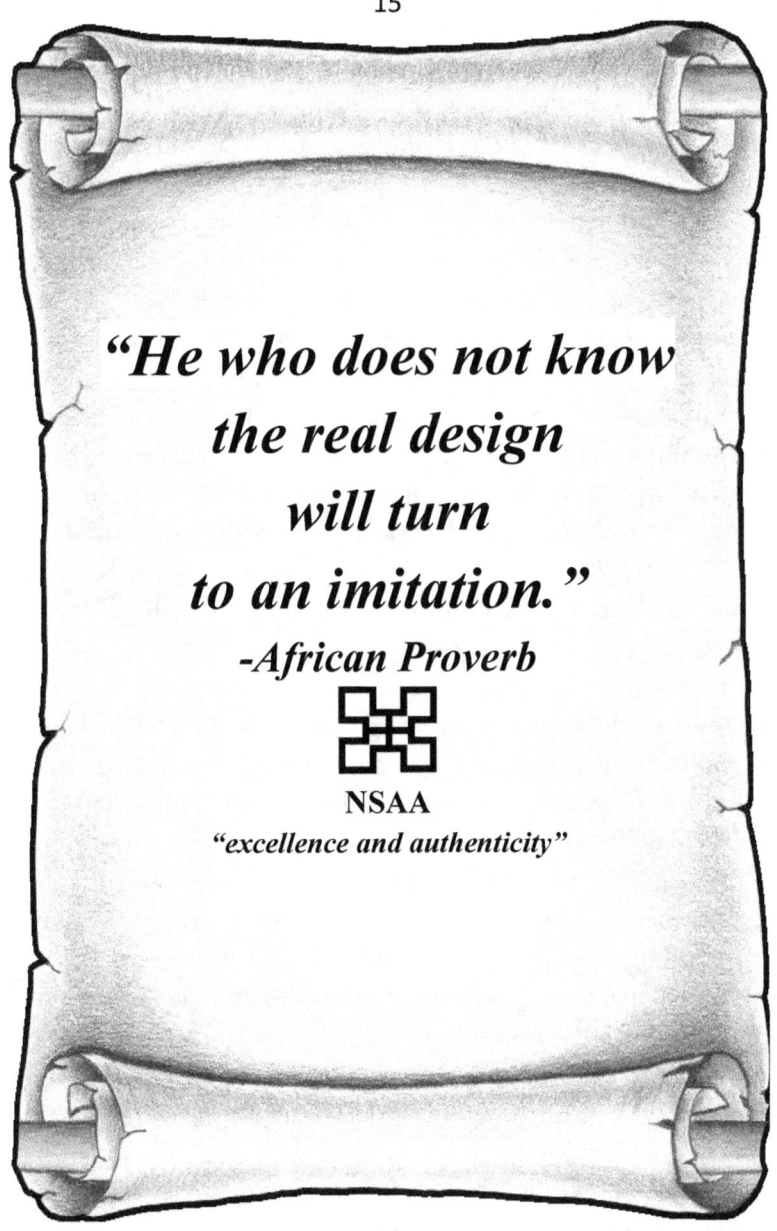

anyone can tell you what your culture is and have you believing that the ways of your people are degenerate, primitive and inferior. *This book will introduce you to the best of your culture which has been intentionally kept from you.*

In addition to understanding what culture is, it is important to understand what racism is and is not. Racism is not a white person calling you the n-word or treating you poorly. It is *prejudice plus power* and it functions as a result of fear and ignorance. As a power dynamic, it affects all areas of people activity, including economics, education, entertainment, labor, law, politics, religion, sex and war. *We do not use racism as an excuse. Racism is, however, a reason why we see so many economic and educational disparities, police brutality, and so much more. It is not all-powerful, but it is pervasive.* If you do not understand racism, what you think you know will only serve to confuse you (Fuller, 1984).

Though it is pervasive, we need not be daunted or discouraged by racism. *Honoring Our Ancestral Obligations requires "a consciousness of victory" as opposed to dwelling on oppression (Asante, 1988).* It requires that we tap into our personal and collective power, harness it and direct it toward transformative ends. Our personal and collective power is greater than racism once we awaken and unify. This is why so much energy is exerted in this society to keep us asleep, disunified and disempowered. *America has tremendous opportunity, but it also has deeply structured inequity. Our task is to take advantage of the opportunity and transform the inequity.*

You will notice that this book contains a number of quotes and African Proverbs. African Proverbs contain the collective cultural wisdom of a people and serve to center us in the best wisdom that our Ancestors consciously sought to preserve.

Honoring Our Ancestral Obligations

> *"Culture provides… a general design for living and patterns for interpreting reality."*
> —Dr. Wade Nobles
> *Psychologist*

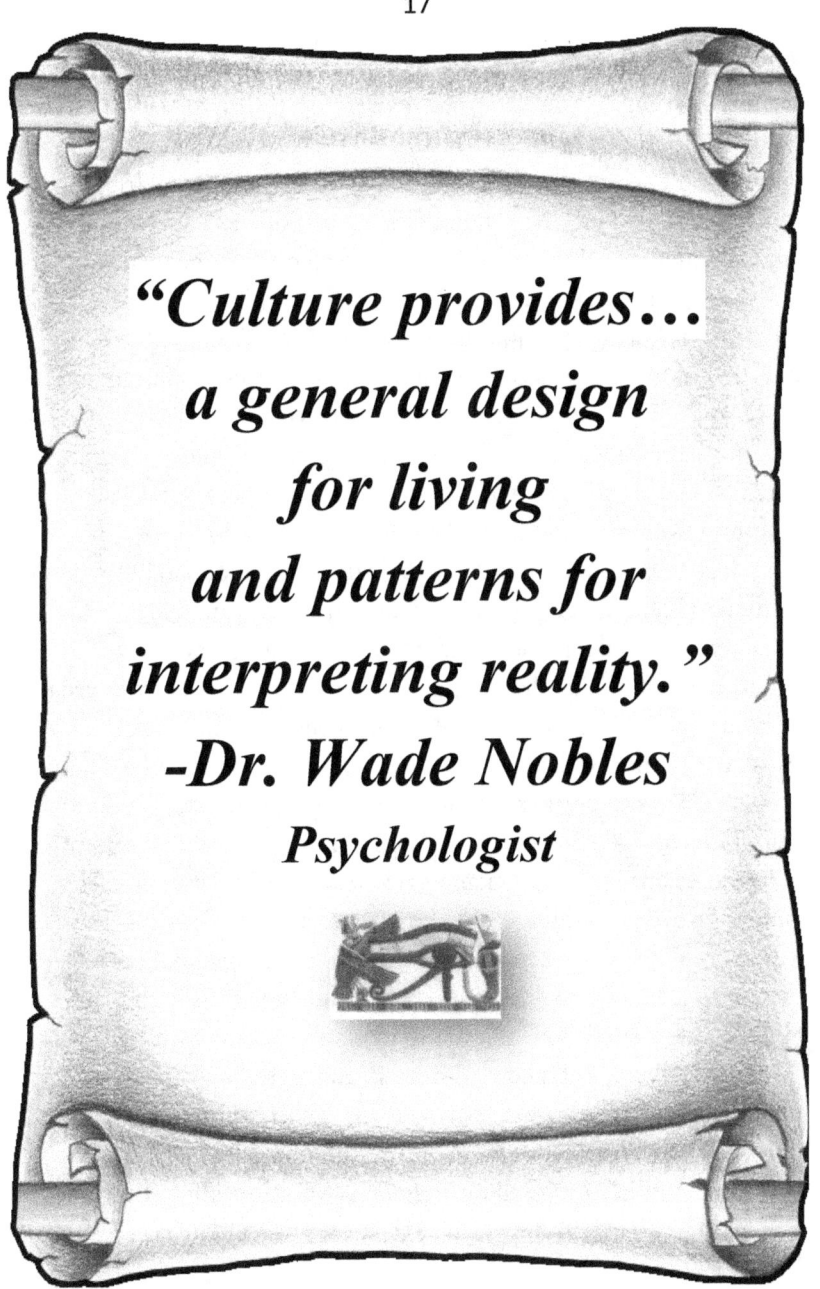

XIIIIXIIIIXIIIIXIIIIX **CHIKE AKUA** XIIIIXIIIIXIIIIXIIIIX

Honoring Our Ancestral Obligations

18

There is an African Proverb which says, "one who knows proverbs soon sets difficult matter aright" (Hilliard, 1987). In addition to proverbs, you will see Adinkra symbols at the beginning of each chapter. Adinkra symbols of West Africa, like other African symbols, contain character traits and deep cultural and spiritual insights which call attention to the direction we must go (Willis, 1995).

When I was a junior in high school, I had a 1.9 GPA. Later, I would go through a dramatic transformation and raise my GPA to a 3.9. But during the difficult years, my GPA was not an indication of my true intelligence. While my grades were low, my potential was sky-high. I have met countless youth in the same situation who are floundering in school and just need someone to recognize their true potential and help them actualize it. This book is a resource that can aid in the process.

Once I became a reader and began valuing books, it was small books like this that transformed my life. Books from great scholars and educators like Baba Zak Kondo, Na'im Akbar, Tony Browder, Amos Wilson, and Jawanza Kunjufu had a profound impact upon me until I could work up to larger books like *The Autobiography of Malcolm X*. Their small books were packed with powerful information and vivid examples, written in clear and compelling language. It is my hope that this book has the same effect on you. I have attempted to make this book as brief but impactful as possible. If this book taps your spirit and touches your soul, don't keep it to yourself. Share with family, friends and acquaintances. **There is an African Proverb which says,** *"If you wish to travel fast, go alone; but if you wish to travel far, go together."* Anything of substance that we have accomplished, we did it *together*. So, if possible, find like-

Honoring Our Ancestral Obligations

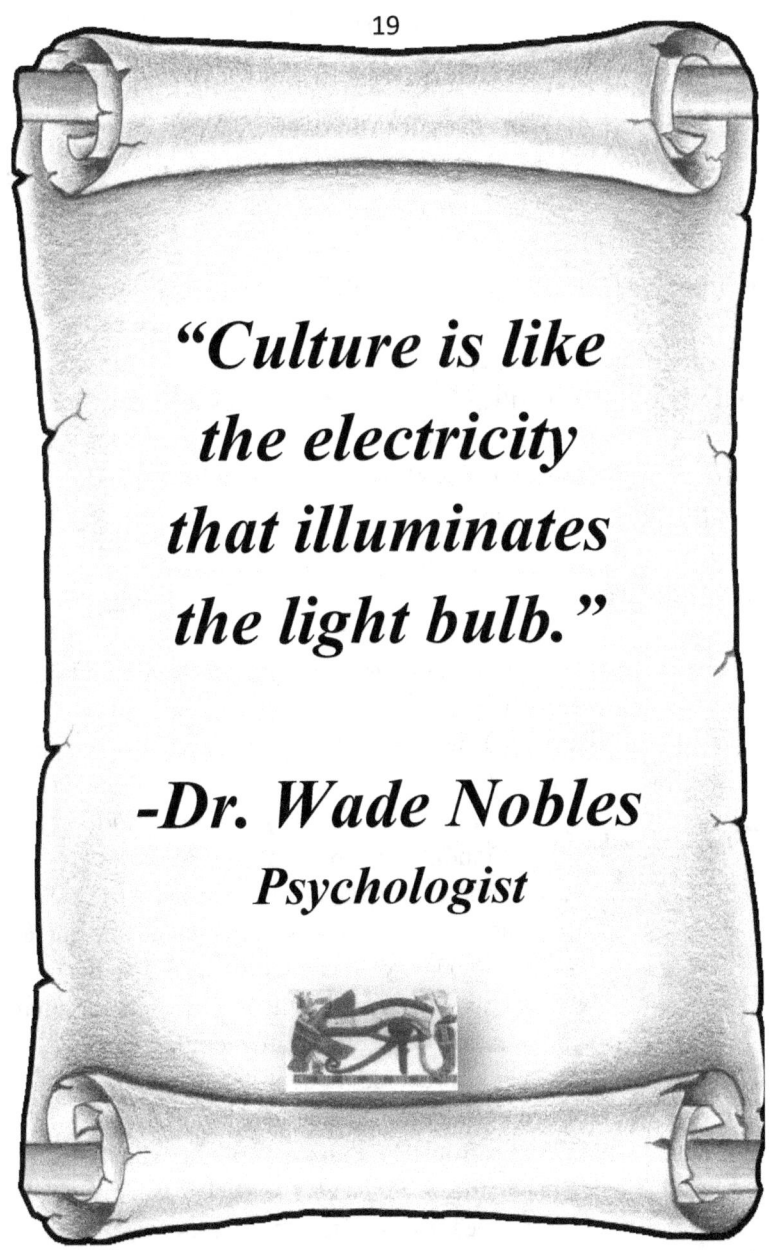

"Culture is like the electricity that illuminates the light bulb."

-Dr. Wade Nobles
Psychologist

CHIKE AKUA

minded brothers and sisters that you can share this book with because you will need others for support on your journey.

Lastly, in this new, revised 4th Edition, we have provided a QR code that, when scanned, allows the reader to see 15 brief video clips about key concepts in this book. This edition has new sections on "Learning and Practicing the Skill of Investing" and "Mastering Our Mental Health." Also, what were called "Chapters" in previous editions, I have termed "Steps" in this edition since the subtitle of the book is "7 Steps to Black Student Success." With each Step we rise individually and collectively in our consciousness (mindset), competence (skill set) and commitment (follow through).

About the Cover

The cover of this book is both deeply significant and symbolic. What thoughts, feelings and/or questions does it evoke within you? The colorful background is kente cloth which originates in Ghana, West Africa. The weaving of kente cloth is a sacred craft and the

cloth was traditionally worn by royalty. Oftentimes, the patterns in kente cloth are symbolic and tell a story of proud African traditions that must be remembered and passed on. Today, you may see African Americans who want to express the beauty of their culture wearing kente cloth outfits or clothes accented with kente cloth to evoke ancestral and cultural consciousness.

The large mask comes from The Empire of Benin, which was a part of what today is Nigeria. The reason the mask was chosen for the cover is because it appears to be a sacred Ancestor looking directly and intently at you to remind you of your obligations to carry on and represent the best of African culture and tradition at a

Honoring Our Ancestral Obligations

time when the worst of the culture has been placed in broad circulation through skillful media manipulation.

The pictures of young people engaged in academic excellence, scientific inquiry and athletics represents those chosen few who have accepted the call of the Ancestors to restore our people to their traditional greatness. These represent courageous young brothers and sisters who are *not afraid to be great*. They achieve against the odds and dare to be outstanding in every way, regardless of what others say. **Will you be one of the chosen few?**

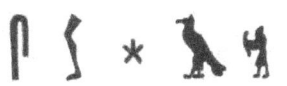

The symbols beneath my name on the front cover are significant, as well.

The symbols are *Medu netcher* writing (often called hieroglyphics), which originated in Nubia (present-day Sudan) and were further developed and popularized in Kemet (present-day Egypt). The symbols spell the word Seba. Seba refers to the Master Teacher. Seba has several meanings, including "teach," "door," and "star." It tells us that the ancient African philosophy of education is that "the teacher opens the door to the Universe so that the student may shine like a star." The first three glyphs by themselves refer to the Seba as a student who serves, stands and shines. My purpose and mission is to be a Master Teacher. But to be a Seba Master Teacher, one must first be a Seba Student who serves, stands and shines.

I would like to thank a very talented and gifted young graphic artist, author, speaker and trainer--Malcolm McRae, who took the concepts I gave him and used his spiritual, cultural and creative consciousness to craft and design such a beautiful and colorful cover that speaks to the spirit of those who see it.

> "I have come here
> to bear witness to the truth
> and to set
> the scales of justice
> in their proper place
> among those
> who have no voice."
>
> **-Prt Em Heru**
> *"The Book of Coming Forth By Day"*
> Circa. 2500 B.C.E.

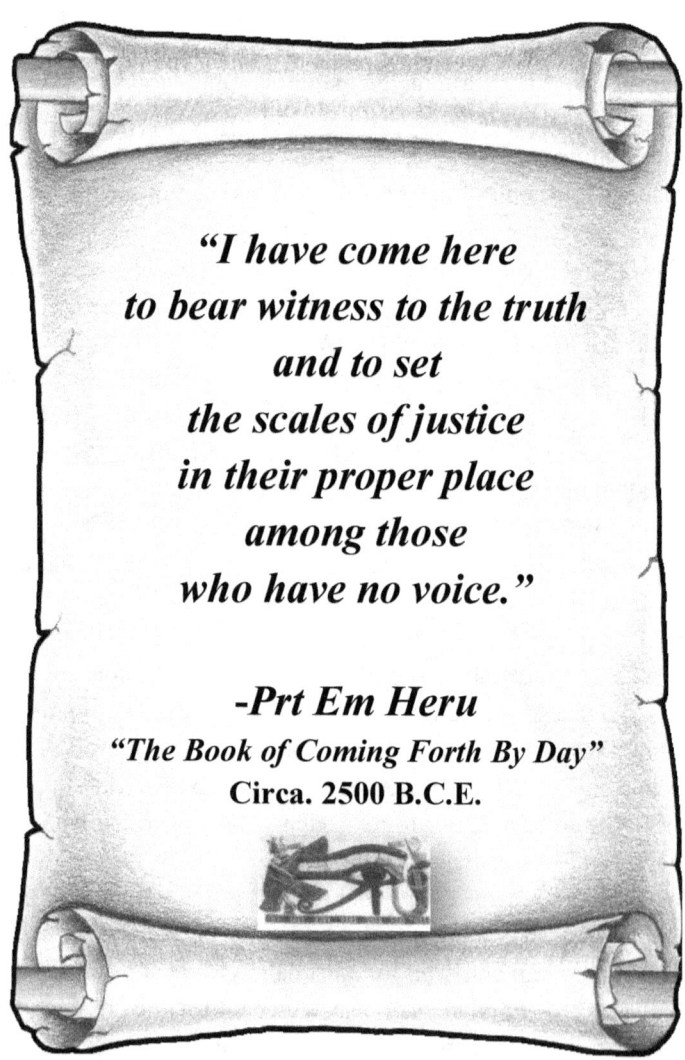

Step 1

Identity Restoration:
Centering Ourselves for the Journey Ahead

We have an Ancestral Obligation to restore our authentic identity.

MATIE MASE
"wisdom, knowledge, prudence"
"what I hear, I keep"

Several years ago, I was logging in to my email account. On the login page was a listing of the days' headlines with a picture in reference to the most important headline of the day. The major news headline read, *"Identity theft is the fastest growing crime in America!"* The picture was a sinister-looking masked-man holding a laptop computer.

As I travel around the country, to dozens of cities per year, speaking to students, teachers and parents, I always ask the members of the audience to raise their hand if they know someone who was a victim of identity theft. Everywhere I have ever asked this, approximately 70-90% of the audience raises their hand.

I was a victim of identity theft and it was not a pleasant experience. Someone captured my personal information and began using my name and my resources to make unauthorized purchases. It can take years to resolve these issues and restore one's identity. Like many others who have been victims of identity theft, I was *confused*, *angry*, and *disillusioned*. It was through this process that what was happening to African American students all over became very clear to me.

In many regards, African American students have experienced <u>cultural identity theft</u> (Akua, 2012). Someone has stolen our story. The aim of cultural identity theft is what Dr. Joyce King calls *identity replacement* (King, 2014). Our story has been replaced with a glorified narrative of pimps, playas, criminals, and thugs. And so we have looked on with deep concern at the onslaught of images which gangsterize and criminalize our Black male children. We have looked on with the same dismay at the manipulation, objectification, and hyper-

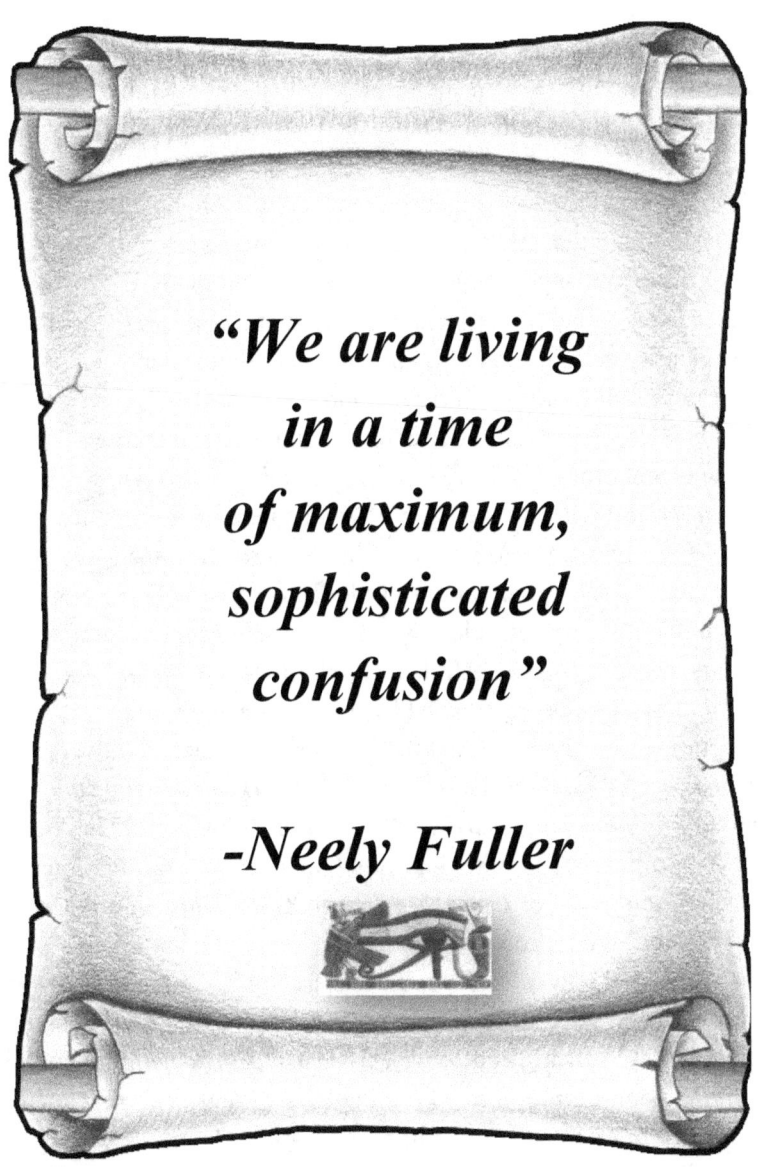

"We are living in a time of maximum, sophisticated confusion"

-Neely Fuller

sexualization of Black females. This creates what Dr. Na'im Akbar has called the *alien* [cultural] identity—an identity that is foreign and alien to our most cherished values and traditions (Akbar, 1998).

I began to realize that the same confusion, anger, and disillusionment that I felt when my identity was stolen, is the same confusion, anger, and disillusionment that many Black students face today in places and spaces that are set up to steal their identity and fail them. So authenticating our identity is paramount today. **Education is identity restoration.**

Gaining access to our bank accounts, social media accounts and other important accounts requires *multi-factor authentication* wherein we must provide an email address, a password, a checkbox to prove you're not a robot, a security code, etc. As such, there are multiple factors that indicate our authentic culture. And today, we must authenticate our identity to gain access to the Ancestral well of knowledge, insight and solutions without being swayed by the weapons of mass deception and weapons of distraction that have been deployed against us. As Neely Fuller has indicated, *"We are living in a time of maximum, sophisticated confusion"* (Fuller, 1971).

So the first step in Honoring Our Ancestral Obligations is the conscious act of **Cultural Identity Restoration.** You must be taken through a process to understand who you are, *whose* you are, where you come from and where you're going. If you don't cultivate your *authentic* identity, society will assign you an *alien* identity. *An* <u>authentic</u> *identity is an identity which contains values and habits to help you become successful and reproduce the best of your culture. An* <u>alien</u> *identity is one which has been skillfully and carefully crafted and imposed upon you for the purpose of manipulation, exploitation and suppression of your greatness.* It is an identity that is foreign to your cultural traditions and values. It comes with a barrage of images of underachievement, irresponsibility, poverty, as well as foolish, violent and self-destructive behavior for the purpose of reproducing those realities in our communities.

In traditional African culture, good character is critically important. Character is the development of morals, values, and codes of conduct. In West Africa, among the Yoruba, good character was referred to as *Iwa* (pronounced "ee-wah"). In his book, *Iwa: A Warrior's Character*, Mwalimu Baruti tells us that good character was of supreme importance. It becomes a driving force which directs thought and action (Baruti, 2010). But, have you ever seen your peers or others who look like you, acting like they have *lost their minds*? Have you ever found yourself acting out of an alien identity rather than an authentic identity? To lead a life of success and fulfillment requires that we center ourselves.

Centering Ourselves for the Journey Ahead

Success requires a plan of action. You've probably heard it said that, "If you fail to plan, you plan to fail." In order to find success, we must chart a path but also be mindful of the pitfalls that may be placed in our path. The following series of diagrams will help us to see how to chart our path and also the pitfalls to look out for.

Picture a circle with a dot in the middle. The dot in the middle is you. Everything within the boundaries of the circle represent the cultural morals and values and actions that produce everything you want in life. As you journey through life, if you stay within the sacred circle, you are *centered* (Asante, 2007) — you have access to love, joy, peace, safety, prosperity, power, etc. All this is at your disposal, as long as you remain *centered*.

Honoring Our Ancestral Obligations

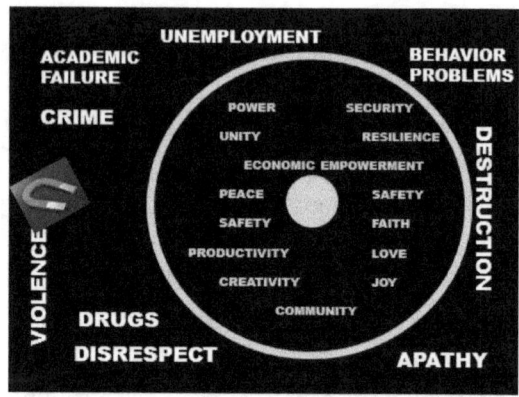

However, there are many forces and factors in society that seek to seductively *de-center* us and draw us away from our power (Asante, 2007). They are like a magnet. Just like a magnet attracts metal, the forces and factors in society attract us based on our vices. *Once we are de-centered and drawn outside of the sacred circle, we are now vulnerable to all the ills of the world that we do not want:* academic failure, behavior problems, disrespect, depression, deception, destruction, violence, etc.

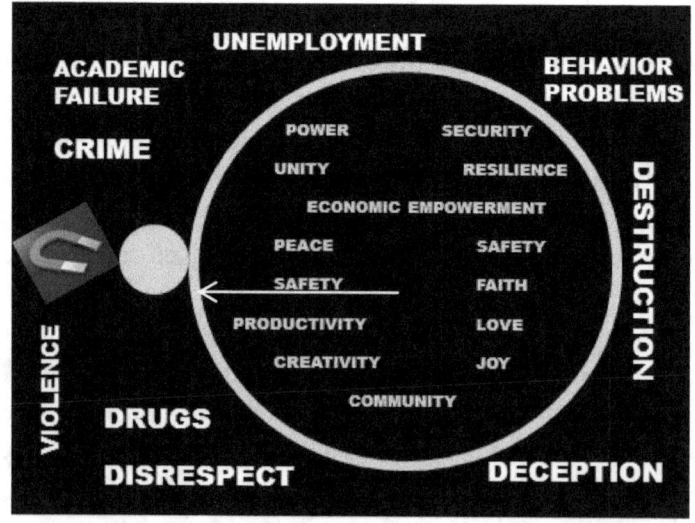

Because our history, culture and identity were taken from us, *we have become de-centered. Now we must become re-centered. Dr. Molefi Asante suggests that our power is in*

remaining centered in the best of our culture and perspectives (Asante, 2007). This is our place of power. This does not mean that we shouldn't learn about others. *We should understand and appreciate other cultures while remaining rooted in our own.*

A deep understanding of family history helps mold and shape identity. There is your immediate family history and there is the extended history of your people. An understanding of both of these histories is essential for you as you grow into a productive adult.

In most schools across the country, we are not taught the true history and culture of African people. As Dr. Asa Hilliard noted, "the education of African people is accomplished in systems that take us far away from ourselves" (Hilliard, 1997). This is one reason why we must do sankofa. The West African concept of *sankofa* means, "return and retrieve it" (Karenga, 1998). It is the perennial quest to retrieve the best of one's history, culture, and legacy and remain grounded in it. It is represented by the mythical sankofa bird which turns its head all the way around to look behind itself. It is also represented in a heart-shaped symbol, perhaps because the heart of our power lay in understanding who we are and where we came from. This concept is further illuminated in the African proverb which says, "To go back to the past is the first step forward."

However, there are three critical mistakes that many teachers and professors make consistently relative to teaching about the contributions of African people to humanity:

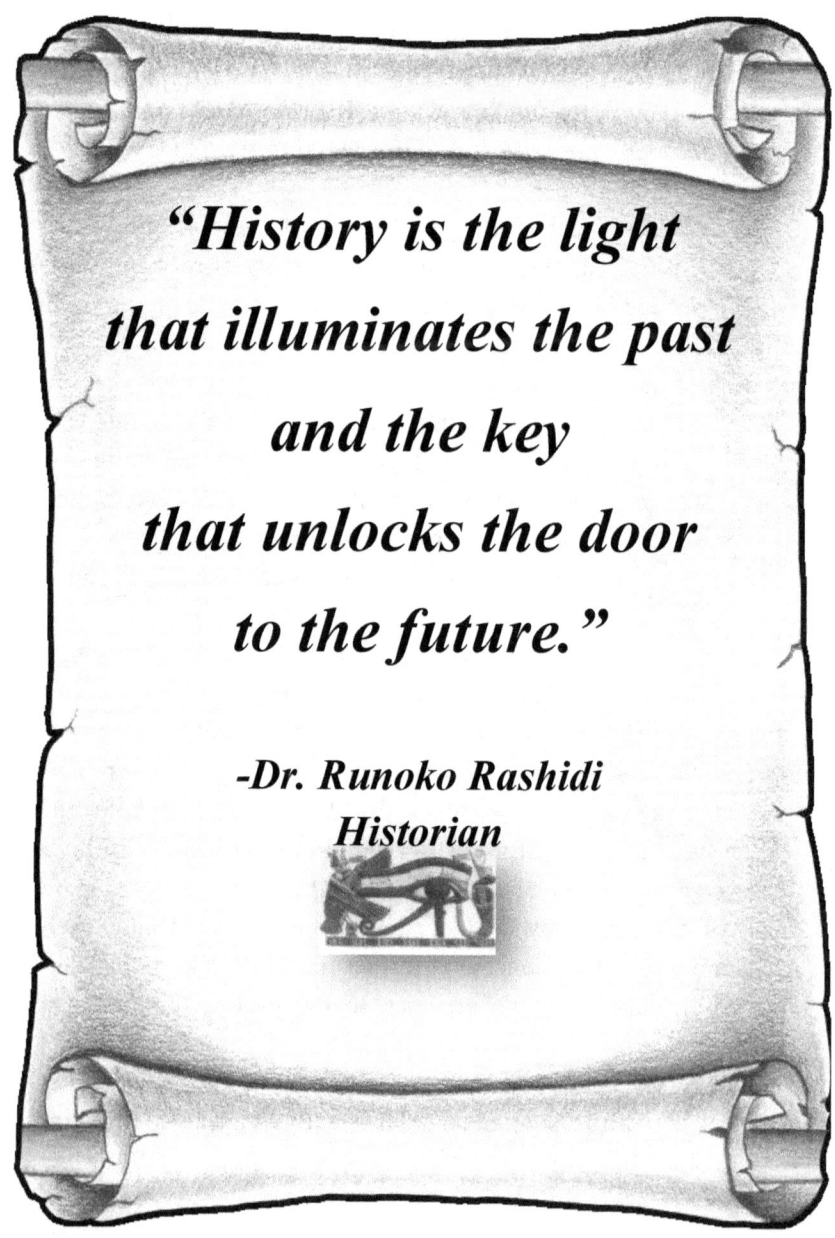

"History is the light that illuminates the past and the key that unlocks the door to the future."

-Dr. Runoko Rashidi
Historian

1. They relegate such teaching to February, the shortest month of the year.
2. They begin the story of African people with the period of enslavement or civil rights, leaving out thousands of years of independent African excellence and achievement.
3. They relegate the teaching of African contributions to the social studies/civics/history class.

As a result of these critical mistakes, many Black people have *cultural amnesia*. Of course, amnesia is a severe loss of memory. This loss of cultural memory is what has allowed others to supplant an *authentic* African identity with a self-destructive, *alien* identity. Dr. Runoko Rashidi tells us that, "History is the light that illuminates the past and the key that unlocks the door to the future." Often the story of African people, their culture, and their history either gets told incorrectly or not at all (Akua, 2012, p. 114).

Authentic v. Alien Cultural Images

A few years ago, I asked a group of students, "What are the predominant images you see of Black people in the media? In other words, how are Black people often portrayed in movies, TV programs, and music videos?" The students' responses were not surprising. On one side of the board I put "Black Male" and the other side of the board I wrote "Black Female." These are the answers the students gave in all five classes that I asked:

Black Male	**Black Female**
Violent	Bad Attitude
Criminal	Loud
Disrespectful	Teen/Unwed Mothers
Pimps & Playas	Welfare Mothers
Deadbeat Dads	Video Vixens

"Wait a minute," I said to each class. "I didn't say to name all of the *negative* images. I just said name the predominant images."

"We did!" they said. So then I asked another question: "Well, what percent of Black people do you think act like these images that you say you see in the media?" The students' responses can only be described as shocking: *Most of the students said they thought 70-90% of Black people acted like the negative images they saw in the media.*

"Wow!" I said shaking my head. "They got you!"

"What do you mean Mr. Akua?!" they asked.

"In fact, it is the exact opposite! 70-90% of Black people are hard-working people who get up everyday and go to work to provide for their families or go to school to better themselves. It's probably closer to 90%. But the majority of media images makes you *think* that Black people are crazy with violent, ignorant, impoverished images. You then begin to act according to those images, thinking that's what it means to be Black."

In addition, these alien images serve to justify anti-Black racism and white terrorism. From 2012-2016, the nation was rocked with the highly publicized and improperly prosecuted murders of Trayvon Martin (Sanford, FL), John Crawford

(Dayton, OH), Jordan Davis (Jacksonville, FL), Eric Garner (NY), Mike Brown (Ferguson, MO), Tamir Rice (Cleveland, OH), Walter Scott (North Charleston, SC), Sandra Bland (Hempstead, TX), Freddie Gray (Baltimore, MD), Keith Scott (Charlotte, NC), Alton Sterling (Baton Rouge, LA), Philando Castille (Minneapolis, MN), and Botham Jean (Dallas, TX), just to name a few.

Since the above murders were improperly prosecuted, it set the stage for the uprisings that occurred in the spring and summer of 2020 with the murders of Breonna Taylor, Ahmaud Arbury and George Floyd. These murders sparked national and international outrage and uprisings.

Questions about how Blacks are portrayed in media are very important questions because *many Black males are portrayed as violent, criminal, sexually irresponsible men who sleep with, manipulate and exploit as many women as possible. Many Black women are portrayed as loud, ignorant, manipulative and sexually promiscuous. This kind of behavior is not a part of our authentic cultural tradition.*

Often when we sit down to watch TV or a movie, we are seeking to be entertained. We are relaxed and tend not to want to think deeply about what we are viewing. What we fail to realize is that *every* program and commercial contain deeply persuasive cultural, social and spiritual messages. These messages are dropped right into the subconscious mind.

Critical Thinking to Reclaim Consciousness

When someone has been knocked unconscious due to a staggering blow or accident, first responders and medical professionals always attempt to revive the person and bring them back to consciousness. To bring us back to consciousness from the staggering blows of racism, miseducation and media manipulation, I have developed the Akua Media Rating Scale.

Honoring Our Ancestral Obligations

How did we go...

From Kings and Queens to criminals and crackheads?

From Pyramid Builders to pimps and playas?

From Mothers and Fathers of Civilization to welfare mothers and deadbeat dads?

From thought leaders to just... thots?

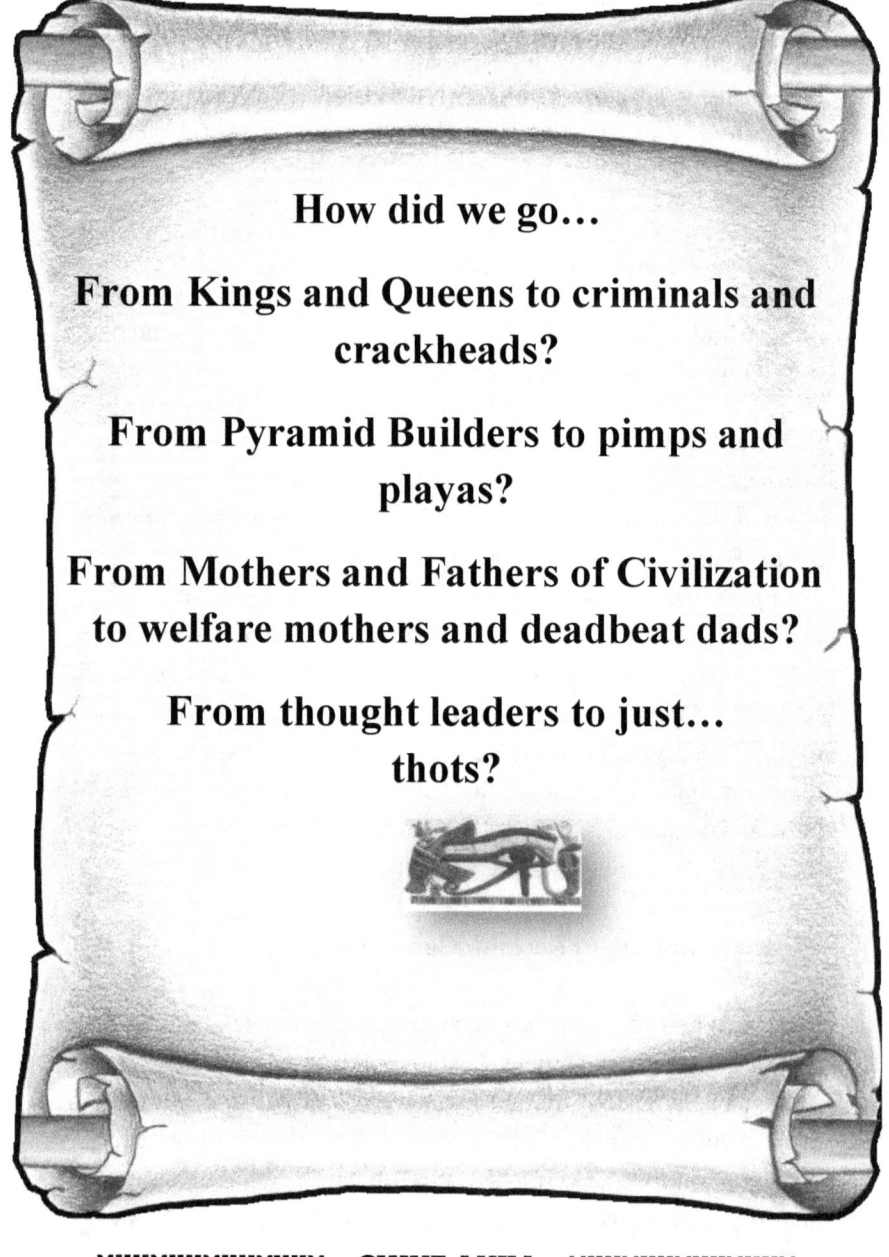

Honoring Our Ancestral Obligations

The number of likes a video, song or post receives on social media or the ratings a show receives on TV does not indicate the quality of the media we consume. It just indicates how many people liked or loved it. Such measures do not indicate the *quality* of the media we consume. It does not indicate whether it has been created as a reflection of the best of our culture or at least a creative critical analysis of issues we face. Haki Madhubuti asks the question we should all consider: "Is it best for our people?"

As Dr. Maulana Karenga noted, "The first act of a free people is to shape the world in its own image and interest" (Karenga, 1999, p. 50). Are the creative productions that we are a part of truly reflective of our image and interests? This must be carefully considered whenever we consume media.

The Akua Media Rating Scale (AMRS) answers the question, "Is this a *quality* program/movie?" "Does it have culturally authentic, positive themes and images which portray Black people at their best?" You can use the AMRS with your family and friends to rate programs and movies. This will encourage you and your family to look carefully and critically at the images presented in the media. Through this careful and critical analysis, we can see how our thoughts and behaviors are shaped, often unconsciously, by what we view.

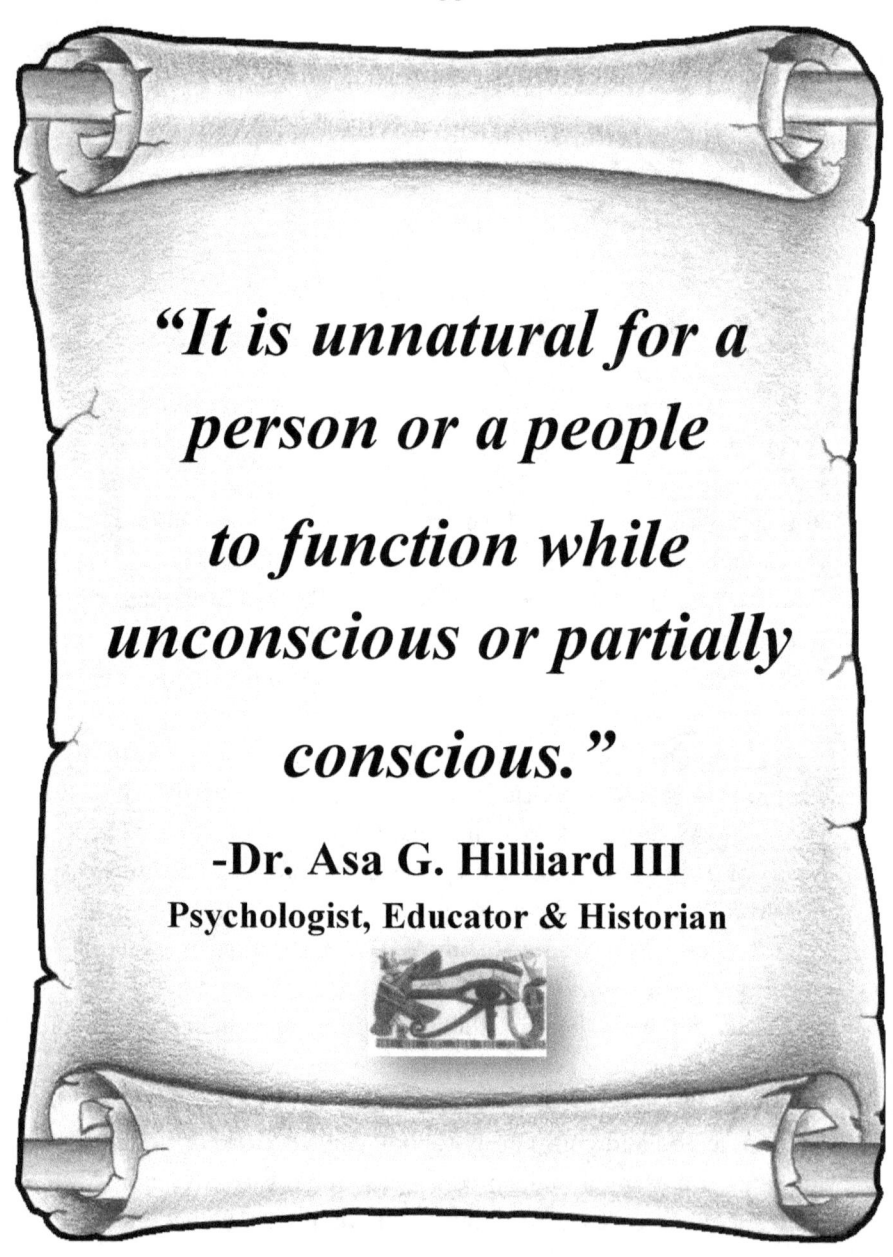

Honoring Our Ancestral Obligations

The Akua Media Rating Scale

Choose a movie or program and rate it from 1-10 (10 being highest) based on the criteria below, then total the score out of 100.

Movie/Program: _____
Category: drama, comedy, action, romance, horror: _____
Starring Actors/actresses: _____

____ 1. What image of Black Manhood is presented?

____ 2. What image of Black Womanhood is presented?

____ 3. What image of Black Family Life is presented?

____ 4. There is no unnecessary profanity spoken or implied (rate a 10 if no profanity).

____ 5. There are no explicit/unnecessary sex scenes (rate 10 if there are no sex scenes).

____ 6. The movie/program had a good message *which was not overshadowed by negative images.*

____ 7. The main character(s) operate with a sense of high moral values or undergo a change in the course of the movie/program which leads them in the right direction.

____ 8. The movie/program did not present negative images of Black people.

____ 9. The main characters could be considered "healthy" mentally, emotionally, culturally, and spiritually.

____ 10. This movie/program inspired me, raised my level of consciousness, or made me think deeply and truthfully about the issues it dealt with..

____ **TOTAL**

Would you recommend this movie/program to others? Explain why or why not? _____

XIIIIXIIIIXIIIIXIIIIX   **CHIKE AKUA**   XIIIIXIIIIXIIIIXIIIIX

WHO ARE WE?

*We are mothers and fathers,
sisters and brothers,
friends and neighbors
who know how to help others.
We are doctors, lawyers, and engineers,
ministers, pastors, and spiritual seers,
educators, counselors,
and business owners,
accountants, dentists,
and even organ donors,
craftsmen, plumbers, and
computer technicians
architects, builders
and also electricians.
We are extraordinary people
with an extraordinary history,
raising families
to leave a lasting legacy.*

-Dr. Chike Akua

We should be just as thoughtful and critical of the music we listen to. ***Music has been scientifically proven to change moods, influence and even alter behavior.*** This can be a good thing or it can be negative depending on the music, who made it and who's consuming it. In his revealing book, *Hip-Hop Hypocrisy: When Lies Sound Like the Truth*, Professor Alfred Powell, writes:

> All songs are written in either major or minor keys. Many Old School songs were written in major keys. That's why they sound upbeat and happy. Major Keys make you feel good. Rap, on the other hand, is usually written in minor keys. Halloween music and music written for horror movies and dramas are written in minor keys. Minor keys make you feel suspenseful, scared, moody, depressed, violent, aggressive, angry, frustrated—basically the lower emotions which…keep us focused on survival thinking v. higher order thinking (Powell, 2004, p. 99).

This is not an attempt to condemn all Hip Hop music. I grew up on Hip Hop from my teens into young adulthood and still listen to some of it. As a matter of fact, ***it was hip-hop music from groups like Public Enemy, Arrested Development, KRS-ONE and X-Clan that sparked my social, political, historical and cultural consciousness.*** Their music had a strong message about Black consciousness and Black Power that fueled my desire to read more and become a teacher, researcher, lecturer, and author. But far too often the artists who have a positive, thought-provoking, uplifting message do not receive the recording contracts that give them wide exposure. Artists who promote negative, anti-African, self-destructive, and anti-human messages are usually awarded the contracts that yield them worldwide exposure and appeal. Professor Powell goes on to tell us:

> Repetitive TV viewing leads to **copy cat behaviors**. Hip Hop video editors often use rapid, chaotic editing techniques, such as quick cuts from scene to scene and zooms in and out, which overloads the viewer's brain…What's more, *the quick cut technique enables producers to hide even more offensive images* frame by frame to have a subliminal impact. Likewise, during the production of an album, offensive lyrics can secretly be inserted in tracks. Young people haven't yet developed the ability to sort out fantasy from reality. Children act out scenes they see on TV (Powell, 2004, p. 107-108).

I developed the **Akua Music Rating Scale** so we can use the same set of criteria from the Akua Media Rating Scale to evaluate music that we used to evaluate movies and TV programs. With this thought in mind, check out the music you and your friends listen to and do the Akua Music Rating Scale with them. Try to let them draw their own conclusions without seeming judgmental or as if you're trying to get them to stop listening to it. Use the Akua Music Rating Scale to think critically, analytically and reflectively about what you and others listen to. Use it to determine what is *healthy* to listen to. Use it to determine how certain types of music that receive wide distribution affect people's thoughts, emotions and actions.

Honoring Our Ancestral Obligations

41

Akua Music Rating Scale

Choose a song and rate it from 1-10 (10 being highest) based on the criteria below, then total the score out of 100.

Song/Album: _____
Category: Hip Hop, pop, R & B, Jazz, Gospel, etc.: _____
Artist:_____

____   1. What image of Black Males is presented.

____   2. What image of Black Females is presented?

____   3. What image of the Black Family is presented?

____   4. What image of Black Youth is presented?

____   5. What image of the Black Community is presented?

____   6. There is no unnecessary profanity spoken or implied (rate a 10 if no profanity).

____   7. There is no explicit/unnecessary sexual suggestions spoken or implied (rate 10 if there are no sex scenes).

____   8. The song has a good message *which was not overshadowed by negative images.*

____   9. The video contained positive uplifting images of Black People.

____   10. This song/album inspired me, raised my level of consciousness, or made me think deeply and truthfully about the issues it dealt with.

____   **TOTAL**

*Would you recommend this song/album to others? Explain why or why not?*_____

XIIIIXIIIIXIIIIXIIIIX   **CHIKE AKUA**   XIIIIXIIIIXIIIIXIIIIX

Lastly, *when it comes to media mindfulness, you should be keenly aware of the misuse of social media.* **You should be very thoughtful and careful about your online identity because all of your words and behaviors are being tracked.** Young people without proper supervision have been known to bully and threaten their peers by posting videos to social media. Young people without proper supervision have also been known to post inappropriate pictures.

Once these things have been posted, their online identity is set and sealed because it can all be traced. One of the first things college admissions officers and employers do is they "Google" the names of their applicants and look them up. If inappropriate pictures, videos, or social media posts come up, they could be denied admission or employment because colleges, universities, and employers are selective about who they want to represent their institution or business.

Questions for Thought, Reflection & Discussion

1. What is cultural identity theft?
2. Define the following terms and give examples:
    a. Centered
    b. De-centered
    c. Re-centered
3. Compare and contrast the *authentic* identity with the *alien* identity.
4. Explain what *sankofa* means?
5. Name some mistakes that are made when teaching about Black history and culture.
6. Choose a TV program or movie and rate it using the Akua Media Rating Scale.
7. Choose a song by a Black artist and rate it using the Akua Music Rating Scale

Step 2

Education for Liberation: Understanding the Power of Our Collective Story

We have an Ancestral Obligation to pursue education for liberation.

SANKOFA
"return and retrieve it"

44

To Honor Our Ancestral Obligations, we must place heavy emphasis on an understanding of education and history for the purpose of building a firm foundation for identity. And, as we will see later, it leads to having a powerful vision for your destiny. This is why an Afrocentric or African-Centered Education (ACE) is helpful. Afrocentric or African-Centered Education (ACE) means, *centering ourselves in the best of our culture to examine and analyze information, meet needs and solve problems in our communities* (Akua, 2019).

There are fifteen elements of African-Centered Education (ACE):

1. ACE (African-centered or Afrocentric Education) places Africa, African people, and African points of view at the center of all things studied.
2. ACE helps students critically examine how the subject or object of study is related to the image and interests of Africa and African people.
3. ACE requires an African value system, that is, one rooted in African culture.
4. ACE requires the restoration of African identity and history.
5. ACE taps into the spirit of the students.
6. ACE requires a sharp orientation toward social justice.
7. ACE requires methods that are unique and indigenous to the nature and needs of African students.
8. ACE requires a relentless quest for agency (power) and a consciousness of victory.
9. ACE asks this simple question of all things: "Is it good or best for African people?"
10. ACE requires an understanding of the *Pan-African* perspective (that all African people are one people wherever they are, whether in Africa, the Americas, the islands of the Caribbean, Europe, Asia, etc).
11. ACE promotes understanding and appreciation for *all* cultures.

12. ACE requires an understanding of cooperative economic empowerment strategies to raise capital and consciousness.
13. ACE prepares students for *sovereignty* (complete control of our own resources, lives, countries and communities
14. ACE requires *social-emotional learning* modalities to resolve the intergenerational and multigenerational unaddressed trauma experienced during the *Maafa* (the catastrophic interruption of African sovereignty and civilization) by way of racism, family separation, fixed poverty, incarceration, physical, emotional and sexual abuse, miseducation, etc.
15. ACE prepares students to defend what we have developed and protect what we have produced) (Akua, 2019).

Far too often, we are centered in European culture and values and use that lens to examine and analyze information. Additionally, we are trained to meet needs and solve problems for communities other than our own using theories and philosophies not our own.

If you attend a school that does not provide an education that centers you in the best of your culture and teaches you how to meet needs and solve problems in your communities, then you will need to do as Dr. Molefi Asante has suggested and **take two sets of notes** in class. The first set of notes is based on what the teacher or professor assigns. The second set of notes is based on the views, values, standpoints and perspectives of your Ancestors and contemporary Black scholars who follow the best tradition of our Ancestors. This often requires you to read books that the teacher or professor did not assign.

To give you an idea of the accomplishments and contributions of African people that have been systematically kept from African people, consider the fact that African people gave the world profound knowledge and understanding of reading and writing, language and literature, agriculture and astronomy, architecture and engineering, mathematics and medicine, civilization and spirituality, science and technology, and much, much more (Finch, 1998).

The vast majority of this information does not make it to the curriculum of most schools and school systems, even the elite private, charter schools, colleges and universities. And oftentimes, those scholars and researchers who engage in such research often find themselves fighting to keep their jobs in systems of schooling that do not support such research.

There was a time when Black people led the world in literary production, scientific innovation and wealth creation. Did you know that:

1. The Ishango Bone found in northeastern Zaire is dated at 25,000 years old and contains markings that clearly demonstrate ancient Africans' understanding of multiplication by doubling and prime numbers (Finch, 1998)?
2. Ancient Africans invented papyrus, the world's first piece of paper (Browder, 1992)?
3. The Ahmose Mathematics Papyrus is the oldest mathematics textbook in the world with examples of algebra, trigonometry, sine, cosine, tangent, cotangent, square roots, area, circumference, volume and much, much more (Obenga, 2004)?
4. The Ahmose Mathematics Papyrus is over 3800 years old and known to be a copy of an older African text (Obenga, 2004)?
5. The Scientific Method is written in the preface of the Ahmose Mathematics Papyrus (Finch, 1998)?
6. Ancient Africans documented their successful medical and surgical methods on papyri (plural form of papyrus) that still exist (Van Sertima, 1992)?

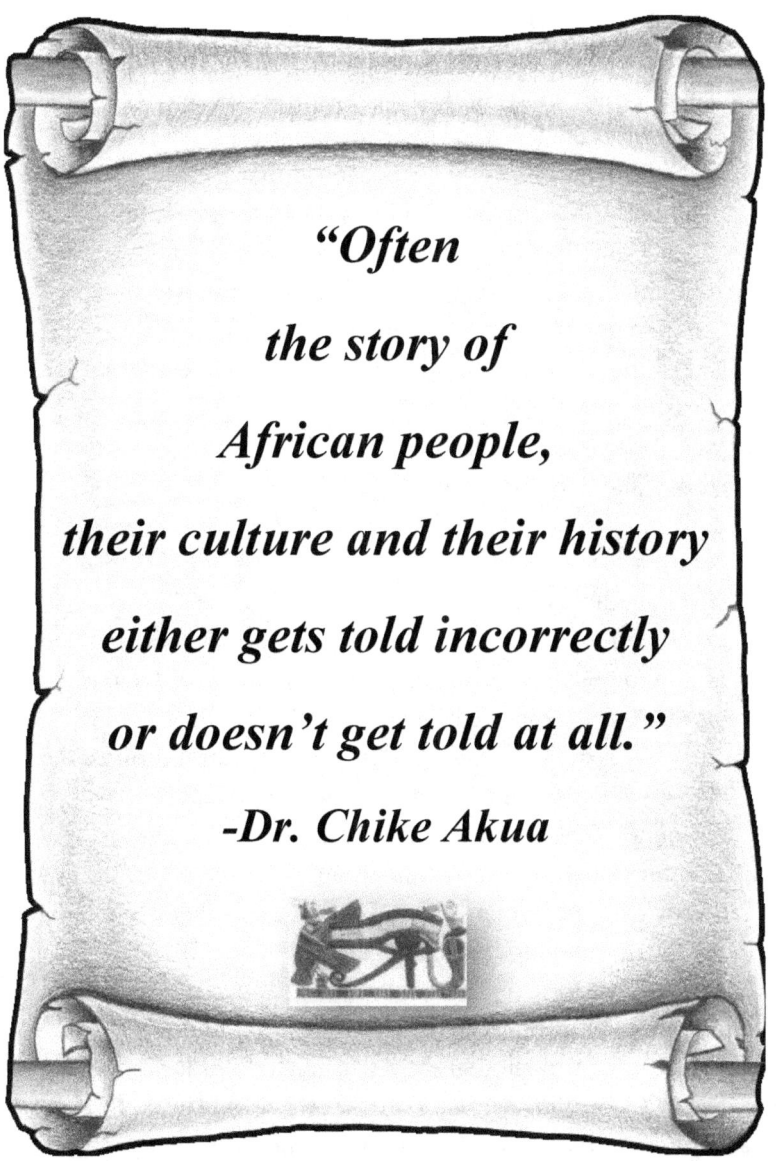

"Often the story of African people, their culture and their history either gets told incorrectly or doesn't get told at all."

-Dr. Chike Akua

7. Ancient Africans documented their success at removing cataracts from the eyes and doing brain surgery over 3500 years ago (Van Sertima, 1992)?
8. The oldest complete text was written by an African man named Ptahhotep 4500 years ago (Hilliard, 1987)?
9. The oldest ship in the world is over 4500 years old. It was dismantled into 1224 pieces and buried behind the Great Pyramid? At the end of each plank of wood were instructions by these brilliant ancient Africans on how to put the ship back together. When archeologists followed the instructions, the boat was over 150 feet long and still seaworthy—meaning, you could put it on the Nile River today and it would float perfectly!
10. The great west African Empires of Ghana, Mali, and Songhoy were thriving when Europe was in the Dark Ages (Maiga, 2009)?
11. Mali and Songhoy were bigger than all of Europe and people came to be educated at the great universities of Djenne, Walata, Gao, and Sankore at Timbuktu (Robinson, 1987)?
12. In West Africa during the Mali and Songhoy Empires, the most valuable commodity along with gold was books (Maiga, 2009, Robinson, Robinson, & Battle, 1987)?
13. The Moors of North Africa brought Europe out of the Dark Ages with their science and technology while also helping to usher Europe into its Renaissance (Rashidi, 2011)?

The historical points enumerated above represent a minute fraction of the body of knowledge that illuminates the incredible accomplishments of African people prior to the slave trade. *This is not hearsay, speculation or opinion. All the contributions mentioned above have been thoroughly documented and proven scientifically with hard, empirical*

Honoring Our Ancestral Obligations

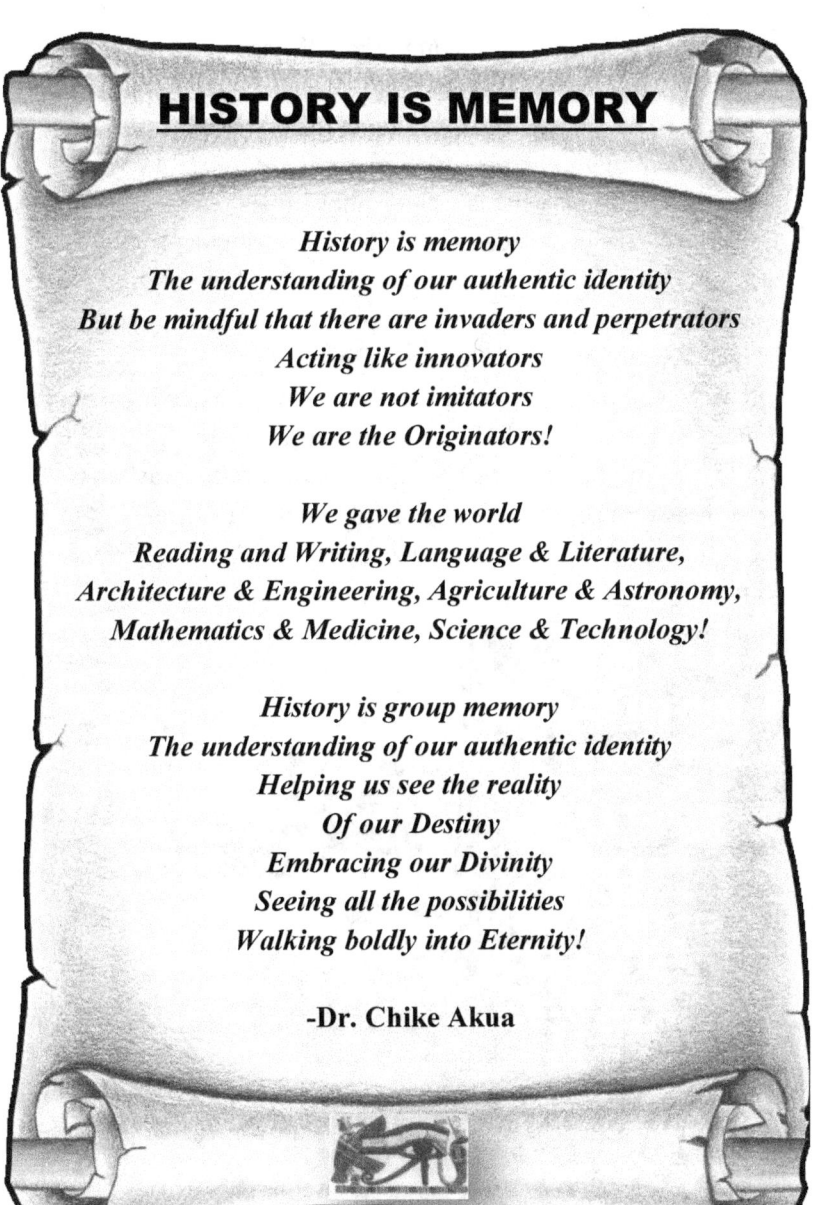

HISTORY IS MEMORY

History is memory
The understanding of our authentic identity
But be mindful that there are invaders and perpetrators
Acting like innovators
We are not imitators
We are the Originators!

We gave the world
Reading and Writing, Language & Literature,
Architecture & Engineering, Agriculture & Astronomy,
Mathematics & Medicine, Science & Technology!

History is group memory
The understanding of our authentic identity
Helping us see the reality
Of our Destiny
Embracing our Divinity
Seeing all the possibilities
Walking boldly into Eternity!

-Dr. Chike Akua

XIIIIXIIIIXIIIIXIIIIX **CHIKE AKUA** XIIIIXIIIIXIIIIXIIIIX

evidence. But as Dr. Joyce King asks, "Whose knowledge is worth knowing (King, 2014, p. *xv*)? Clearly, in many places and spaces, African and African American history and culture is not respected enough to be properly represented.

In addition, what is written above does not even scratch the surface of what African people have contributed or accomplished. Most school children know nothing of this. But they know about and have been taught to respect and revere George Washington and Thomas Jefferson—
both of whom owned African people as slaves. They learn about Napoleon, King Henry VIII, Queen Victoria, Marco Polo, and whole host of other Europeans. This is not to take away from the great things Europeans have invented or accomplished. But to know them and not know what *your own people* have done is criminal.

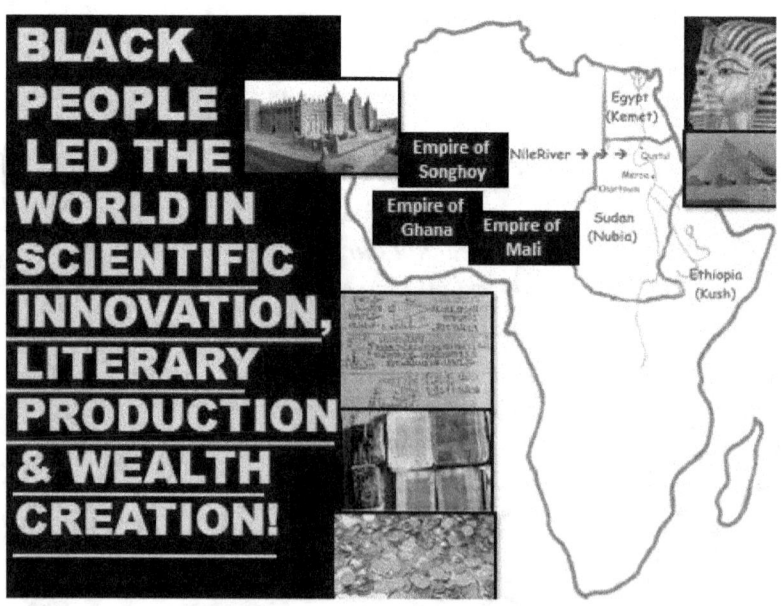

Honoring Our Ancestral Obligations

Dr. John Henrik Clarke
Historian
1915-1998

Dr. Carter G. Woodson
Historian
(1875-1950)

Dr. John Henrik Clarke tells us that "The powerful will never educate the powerless to take their power from them" (Clarke, 1991, p. 18). Dr. Carter G. Woodson must have understood this sixty years prior to Dr. Clarke. Perhaps that's why, in *The Mis-education of the Negro* (1933), he tells us that there are two kinds of education—the kind you are given and the kind you must give yourself (Woodson, 1933).

Current systems of "education" are often structured to keep us dependent on others.

Because of images they have seen in movies and on TV, people often associate poverty, bloodshed, famine and disease with being African. And they often associate being pimps, playas, criminal, thugs, welfare mothers and deadbeat dads with being Black.

History is *memory*, helping us to shape, fashion and form our identity. *Regrettably, the memory of most of our people does not extend beyond that of Dr. Martin Luther King and the Civil Rights Movement or slavery. In addition, most don't even know the truly essential elements of his life and accomplishments. None of this is by chance.* Far too few African Americans have a cultural memory that extends deep enough or back far enough to recapture the cultural wealth that makes us great as a people. Few know details about our wealth, excellence and achievement all over the world prior to our enslavement. It is not by chance that most cannot reconnect to this cultural memory.

XIIIIXIIIIXIIIIXIIIIX **CHIKE AKUA** XIIIIXIIIIXIIIIXIIIIX

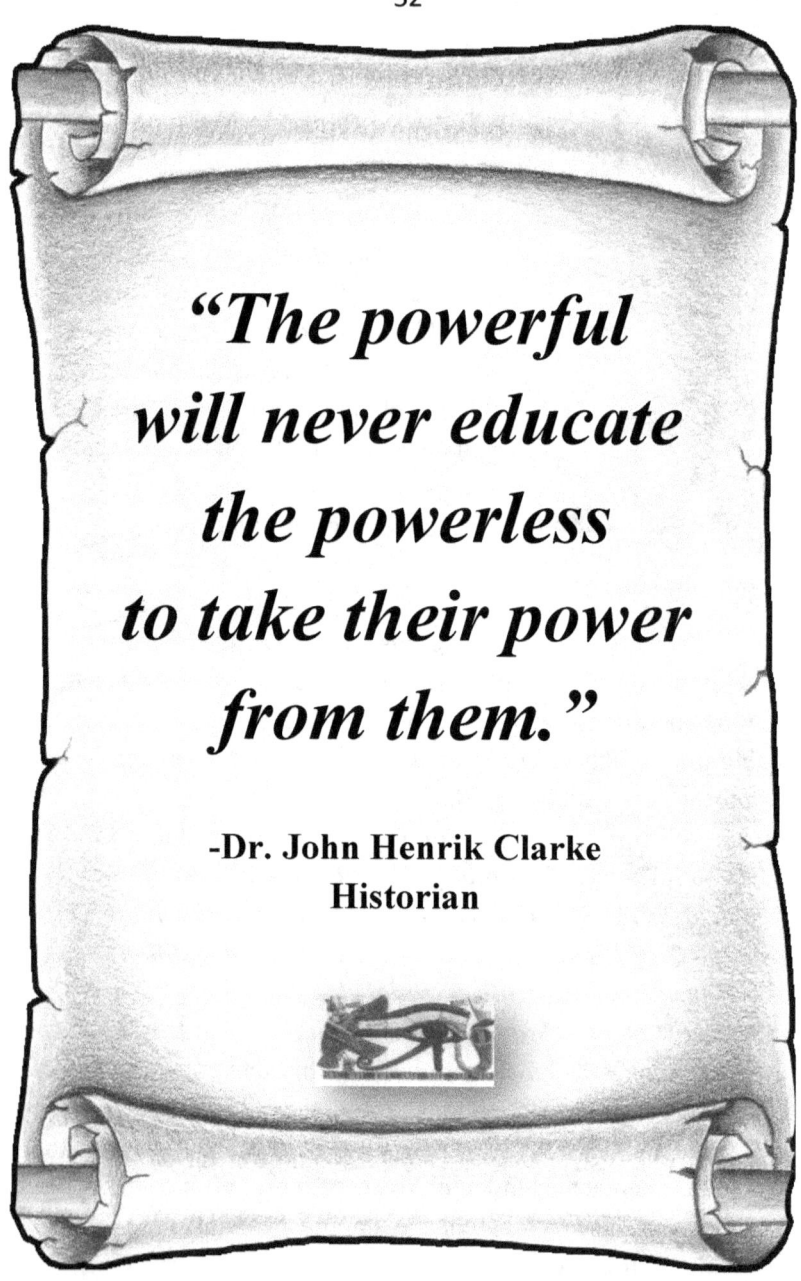

"The powerful will never educate the powerless to take their power from them."

-Dr. John Henrik Clarke
Historian

Honoring Our Ancestral Obligations

Everything about the slavery experience was designed to whitewash our memory because the enslaver understood the power of memory. Dr. John Henrik Clarke observed:

> "The task of Africans at home and abroad is to restore to their memory what slavery and colonization made them forget…in most of Africa, the job was so complete it was tantamount to **a brain transplant**" (Carruthers, 1995).

South African freedom fighter, Stephen Biko, remarked, "The greatest weapon in the hands of the oppressor is the minds of the oppressed." **But what does this have to do with you, your family, and your community?** People who are consciously connected to their culture are able to reproduce the best of the culture and extend the greatness of their culture to a new level (egs. Chinese, Jews, Japanese, British, etc.). Frederick Douglass said, "Knowledge makes a man unfit to be a slave." Marcus Garvey observed, *"We are going to **emancipate ourselves from mental slavery**, for though others may free the body, **none but ourselves can free the mind**…The man who is not able to develop and use his mind is bound to be the slave of the other man who uses his mind."*

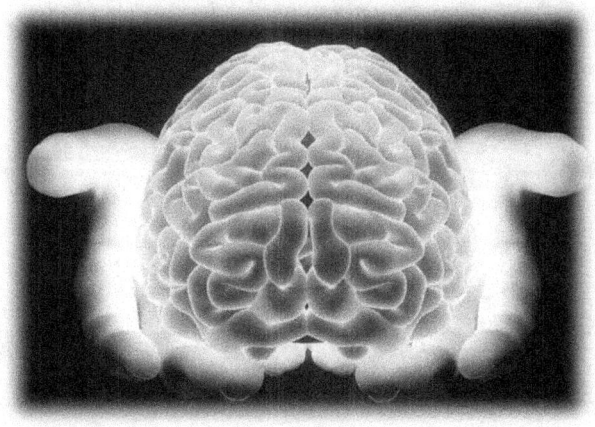

Honoring Our Ancestral Obligations

Do you recognize any of these names?:
- George Washington
- Thomas Jefferson
- John Quincy Adams
- Abraham Lincoln
- Queen Victoria
- Napoleon
- Shakespeare
- Marco Polo

Do you or your child recognize any of *these* names?
- Aha-Mena
- Imhotep
- Ptahhotep
- Queen Tiye
- Amenhotep III
- Hatshepsut
- Sunni Ali Ber
- Ahmed Baba
- Sundiata
- Yaa Asantewaa
- Queen Nzingha
- Marcus Garvey
- Kwame Nkrumah
- Stephen Biko

How is it that you know the heroes of another culture, yet do not know the names or accomplishments of some of the greatest African leaders that we have produced for the world? *How can you study and reproduce the methods of these great leaders, warriors, healers, and nation builders if you have never heard of them?* Perhaps this is why the great Civil Rights Activist, Fannie Lou Hamer said, "Never forget where you came from and always praise the bridges that carried you over" (Karenga, 1998).

As a result of the breakdown of the Black family, there has been a serious crisis in Black manhood and womanhood. As a result of cultural amnesia, we seem to have also forgotten what it means to be a man or woman. This leads to many

misconceptions. In *Visions for Black Men*, Dr. Na'im Akbar (Akbar, 1991) tells us the three stages of development:
1. **Male/Female Stage**: we are born into this world as male or female. This is biologically determined—meaning, a male is born with a penis and a female is born with a vagina.
2. **Boy/Girl Stage**: at a certain point, a male begins to grow into a boy and a female into a girl. A boy and girl has reached a certain level of understanding and discipline only relative to what (s)he wants. So (s)he can be obedient or clean his/her room if (s)he wants to watch TV or go out and play. But his/her level of discipline does not extend far beyond doing what (s)he does to get what (s)he wants.
3. **Manhood/Womahood Stage**: A man or woman is one who has arrived at a particular purpose and destiny. (S)he uses his/her discipline and energy to advance his/her purpose and destiny. T. Garret Benjamin tells us that men and woman *"put down toys and pick up tools."* They use the tools of their mind and skills to build strong families, communities, and businesses.

As a young man, I had to memorize a powerful poem by Haki Madhubuti called "The Book of Life." Here is a brief excerpt that speaks to what we can expect from real men:

You will recognize your brothers by the way they act and move throughout the world.
There will be a strange force about them,
There will be unspoken answers in them...
The way they relate to women will be clean, complimentary, responsible, and with honesty.
The way they relate to children will be strong and soft, full of positive direction.

"In African tradition, manhood and womanhood is not given, but proven."
-Dr. Hassimi Maiga

The Paramount Chief of the Songhoy people of Mali, Dr. Hassimi Maiga, tells us *that in African tradition, manhood and womanhood "is not given, but proven."*

Womanhood, like manhood is not promised. *It is a choice.* Just as there are 20, 30, 40 year old males in the community who know nothing of what it means to be a man, there are also 20, 30, 40 year old females who know nothing of what it means to be a woman.

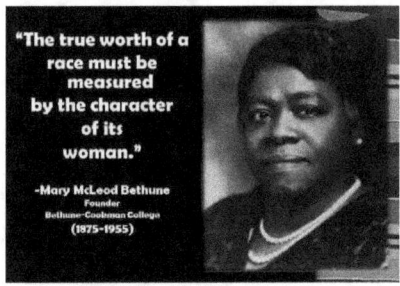

Mary McLeod Bethune, educator and founder of Bethune-Cookman College, once said, *"The true worth of a race must be measured by the character of its woman."* So the dignity and integrity with which a woman carries herself is what sets her apart from others. The dignity and integrity with which a man carries himself is what sets him apart from others. We have an Ancestral Obligation to resurrect the dignity and goddesstry of Black Womanhood and the dignity and majesty of Black Manhood.

The Past, Power & Potential of Historically Black Colleges & Universities (HBCUs)

Now more than ever, a quality education is essential to success in the global economy. Higher education can open the door to opportunity and often greater access to prosperity and security. It is for this reason that the power and potency of Historically Black Colleges and Universities (HBCUs) must be understood and appreciated.

HBCUs have an historical track record of producing outstanding Black professionals. I am a proud graduate of two HBCUs: Hampton University, where I earned a bachelor's degree in English Education and Clark Atlanta University, where I earned a master's degree in education with an emphasis in school counseling.

In addition to producing academic excellence, the spike in highly publicized murders of Blacks by Whites and the increasingly volatile political climate have made HBCUs an even more attractive choice. HBCU attendance has been on the rise because Black students want to be in a physically and culturally safe and supportive environment. PWIs (Predominantly White Institutions) have fewer Black faculty whom students can identify with. The culture and climate at many PWIs can produce feelings of alienation and isolation among Black students. You should go where you are celebrated, not just tolerated.

HBCUs comprise less than 3% of the nations' colleges and universities, but their level of success in preparing and producing Black professionals is unmatched (Fenwick, 2001).

In the book *I'll Find A Way or Make One: A Tribute to Historically Black Colleges and Universities*, Juan Williams and Dwayne Ashley observe:
- HBCUs still graduate **70%** of all Black physicians and dentists.
- HBCUs still graduate **50%** of all Black engineers
- HBCUs produce **50%** of the nation's Black teachers
- Nearly one-third of the bachelor's degrees awarded to Black graduates come from HBCUs.
- Tuskegee University alone graduates more than **80%** of Blacks practicing veterinary medicine.

XIIIIXIIIIXIIIIXIII   Chike Akua, Ph.D.   XIIIIXIIIIXIIIIXIII

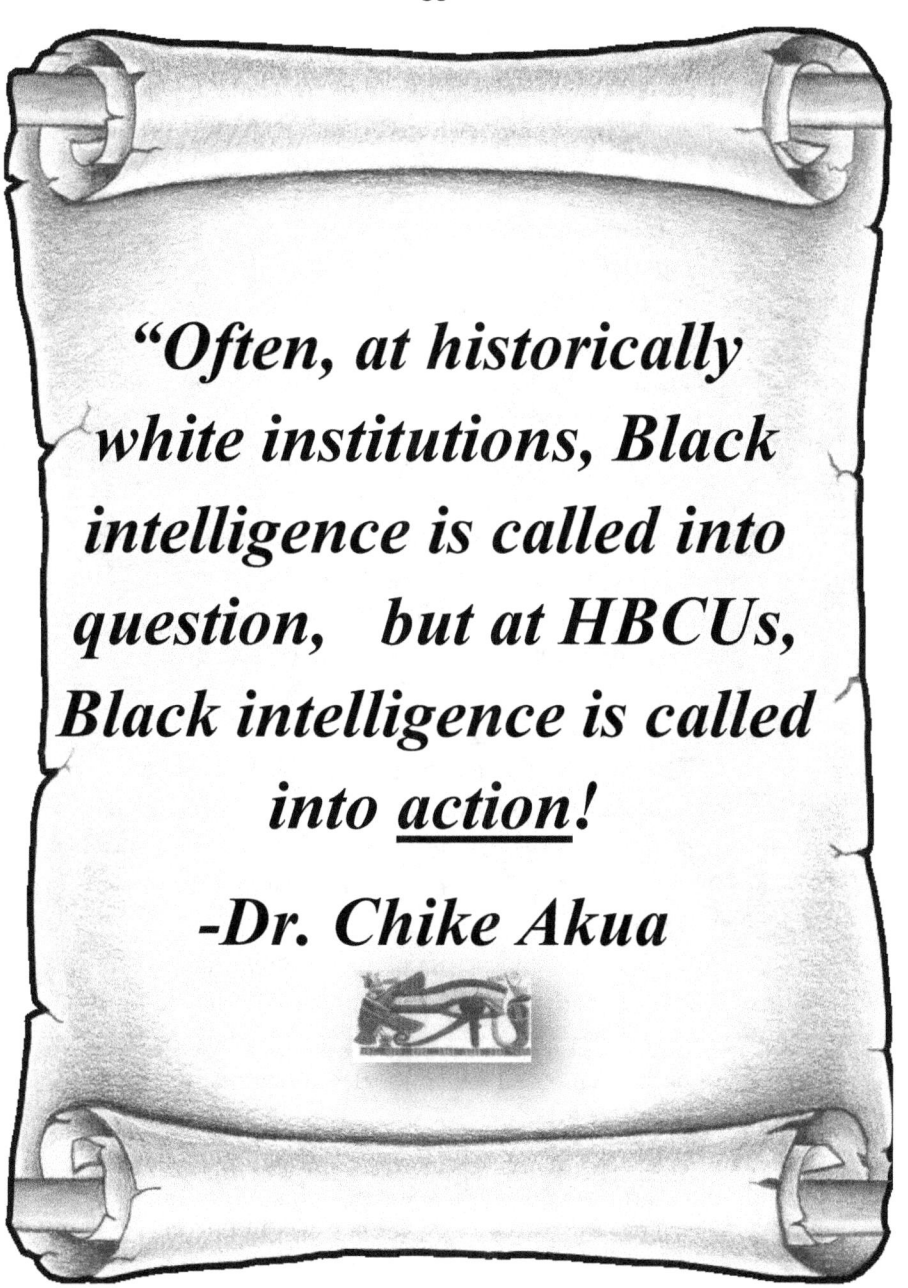

"Often, at historically white institutions, Black intelligence is called into question, but at HBCUs, Black intelligence is called into <u>action</u>!

-Dr. Chike Akua

- North Carolina A&T University is the number one producer of engineering degrees on the undergraduate level awarded to Blacks.
- Black students who attend HBCUs have higher GPAs and higher graduation rates, and higher acceptance rates into graduate and professional schools than their Black peers at predominantly white institutions (Fenwick, 2001).

It is clear that HBCUs have an historical legacy and track record of opening doors of opportunity and producing Black professionals when no one else was interested, willing, or able. Often, at historically white institutions, Black intelligence is called into question, but at HBCUs, Black intelligence is called into *action*!

Black colleges produce great minds and incredible futures. You owe it to yourself to explore the possibility of attending one of the over 100 outstanding HBCUs across the nation—if not for undergraduate education, then for your graduate studies.

Keys to Unlocking Cultural Memory

When we consider the advanced devices of modern technology such as cell phones, computers, tablets, servers, and flash drives, their value is determined based on the amount of memory they can store. ***The more gigabytes and terabytes of memory, the greater the value***.

We have a storehouse of cultural memory that, when accessed, releases and reveals our true potential. But we must retrieve our lost files (history). Systems of miseducation keep this storehouse of cultural memory sealed intentionally because of the fear of our true power.

Family history is critically important, as well. My grandmother grew up during the Great Depression of the 1930s. By the age of 22, she was a widow with four small children ranging in age from 4 months to 4 years old. She was in a helpless and hopeless situation and did not know what to do.

My Grandmother, Robbie C. Ward

She went to a church to see a priest for assistance. After listening to her situation, the priest took one look at her, raised an eyebrow and said suggestively, " I'll take care of you *and* your children." She immediately knew she could not get the help she needed there.

Off she went to the welfare line. In it she saw people who were completely down and out. The spirit of depression was so thick that she vowed never to return after that day—and she never did. She vowed that she would find a way or make a way for herself and her children.--*and that's exactly what she did*. She fulfilled her promise.

She cleaned houses and worked long hours until she stumbled upon an opportunity to go into nurse's training. The only problem was that in order to be in the training program, she could not take her children. She then made one of the most difficult decisions of her life. She placed her children in an orphanage. By this time, my mother was 4 years old, the youngest of the bunch.

My grandmother worked her way through nurse's training and visited her children on weekends and periodically whenever she could, always promising that one day she would come back to take them home. After completing nurse's training, that's exactly what she did.

This story of resilience, tenacity, self-determination and hope is not unique to African American families. Most families have a matriarch or patriarch who did something extraordinary to keep the family together. This story served as an anchoring narrative, a constant reminder to what hard work, faith in God, and pursuit of education can do.

I'll always remember my grandmother telling us, "Baby, make sure you finish school before having children. Giving up my babies was the hardest thing in the world." Neither my sister, nor three brothers had children before finishing school and getting married.

Knowledge of personal family history has the ability to instruct and inspire you. When you know the great sacrifices made to provide for you and how your elders pushed on and persevered to make a way out of no way, you will then feel empowered to make your way through challenging times. You now have a reference point for how to turn challenges and trials into triumph and victory.

Questions for Thought, Reflection & Discussion

1. What is African-Centered Education (ACE)? Which of the fifteen elements of ACE is most important to you and why?
2. There is a list of thirteen little-known facts about African history. Which of these is most interesting to you and why?
3. In what ways have HBCUs demonstrated a track record of success in educating African Americans?
4. Why are more and more Black students choosing HBCUs?
5. Why is your family history important?
6. What important stories have been passed down in your family?

Step 3

Economic Mobilization & Political Participation

We have an Ancestral Obligation to raise capital and consciousness at the same time.

BESE SAKA
"affluence, power and abundance"

Honoring Our Ancestral Obligations

Many of us were told the same three things by our parents about how to be successful. See if you can fill in the blanks:
1. Go to _____.
2. Get your _____...
3. So you can get a good _____ (with _____).

As I speak to parents and students around the country, they always know the exact words that go in the blanks:
1. Go to <u>school</u>.
2. Get your <u>education</u>...
3. So you can get a good <u>job</u> (with <u>benefits</u>).

The problem with this kind of advise is that it is short-sighted and increasingly unrealistic. The economic downturn in America which began around 2008, changed forever the job market and the world of work. Millions of people lost their jobs. Millions of people had homes that went into foreclosure. Millions lost their retirement funds and also declared bankruptcy. So **Honoring Our Ancestral Obligations requires that we examine _greater possibilities_ than simply depending on others to give us jobs that they don't even have for their own people.**

Black people in America have always been the last hired and the first fired with a glass ceiling for those who got their hopes up about rising to the top. This is not to say some have not been successful in corporate America and in government jobs, however, we have not built a thriving *Black* economy that keeps the money in *our* community the way other cultural groups have. This is deeply problematic and requires that there be a shift in the way we prepare for success in a global economy.

Different ethnicities naturally attempt to empower themselves in the market place by dominating a particular industry. In the Black community across America, we find that the Koreans have the Black haircare industry on lock, Arabs and east Indians often own corner stores and gas stations, Jews often control banking, Latinos control construction, whites control most retail stores, and we buy more Chinese food than any other ethnic group. <u>**But what do we own and control???**</u>

Dr. Jawanza Kunjufu tells us that when we accepted integration, **we got what we asked for but lost what we had.** We asked for jobs and received a few more. But we had thriving Black economic districts that we supported all over the country. Just to name a few, there was Black Wall Street in Tulsa, Oklahoma; Rosewood, Florida; Sweet Auburn Avenue in Atlanta, Georgia and Durham, North Carolina, home to a number of Black insurance companies and other thriving Black businesses. We lost virtually all of these due to integration.

Prior to our enslavement, remember, African people led the world in wealth production. We must return to our own and begin to participate in building the Black economy rather than perpetuating unconscious consumerism. Unconscious consumers work to build other people's dreams and make them wealthy.

Do you know what the fastest growing business in America is? Prisons! You need to know the reality and nature of the American prison industrial complex. We were all taught a terrible lie in school. Here it is: The 13th Amendment abolished slavery. This is a very misleading statement. It is not fully incorrect, but it is terribly *incomplete.* **The 13th Amendment reads:**

> *Neither slavery nor involuntary servitude,* ***except as a punishment for crime*** *whereof the party shall have been duly convicted, shall exist within the United States, or any place subject to their jurisdiction.*

Notice that slavery is abolished <u>*except as punishment for a crime in which one has been duly convicted*</u>. Being convicted does not mean one is *guilty*. Black men have been more likely to receive stiffer punishments and convictions for as long as America has existed. Michelle Alexander refers to this in *The New Jim Crow*. To be forewarned is to be forearmed.

Prisons are BIG BUSINESS! Prisons are now privatized and traded publicly on the stock market. This means that when one invests in prisons, like any other stock, they expect to make money. They are making money on the backs of Blacks and other people of color. *The more people that get locked up, the more the investors get paid.*

Do you know who else gets paid? The people who make the orange jumpsuits, flip-flops, prison doors, bars, locks, keys, cameras, surveillance equipment, etc.--ALL GET PAID! All the while, prisoners are doing slave labor for large corporations and receiving slave wages. You must be aware of these kinds of social justice issues.

XIIIIXIIIIXIIIIXIII   Chike Akua, Ph.D.   **XIIIIXIIIIXIIIIXIII**

What is equally as criminal as the prison industrial complex is the lack of consistent, conscious and intentional support Black-owned businesses receive. *The shift in economic consciousness and empowerment that we need requires that we train ourselves to be supporters of Black-owned businesses and also become <u>owners</u>.* Training yourself to be an owner requires that you do a different kind of homework. You must study the lives, mission, and methods of Africans and African Americans who understood and *demonstrated* wealth creation. These are a few of the Black leaders and business people whose *wealth creation* we must carefully study:

- Rameses II
- Sunni Ali Ber
- Mansa Musa
- Jean Baptiste DuSable
- Marcus Garvey
- Booker T. Washington
- Madame C.J. Walker
- A. G. Gaston
- Elijah Muhammad
- John H. Johnson
- S.B. Fuller
- Reginald Lewis
- Robert Smith
- Cathy Hughes
- Oprah Winfrey
- Joe Dudley
- Delxino Wilson de Briano
- Deborah Wilson de Briano
- George Fraser
- Farah Gray
- Earl Graves
- Jackie Mayfield
- Robert Abbott
- Berry Gordy
- Tony Brown
- Byron Allen

When the doors of opportunity were cracked open a little more for Blacks from the 1960s-1990s, we lost our economic foundation in search of employment and acceptance by whites. We could now buy merchandise and food in their stores, sometimes even without poor treatment. A poor child growing up in a Black community prior to integration had the example of being able to see business professionals, doctors, lawyers, carpenters, engineers, constructions workers, ministers, and teachers all living on the same block or within a few blocks of him. However, with integration, a few Blacks who could afford it, were able to move out of Black communities, leaving the communities desolate with crime, drugs, unemployment and few role models.

The Solution

Honoring Our Ancestral Obligations requires cooperative economics. The Honorable Marcus Mosiah Garvey stands as the quintessential historical example of the type of unity and economic development that we need to practice. In the 1920s, with his Universal Negro Improvement Association (UNIA), he built factories, clothing stores, bakeries, and grocery stores, along with a fleet of ships called the *Black Star Line*. The businesses of the UNIA employed over 1000 Black people in New York City alone. They even had a factory which manufactured Black dolls for children! The newspaper of the UNIA, *The Negro World*, was printed in French, Spanish, and English and had a readership of over 200,000 people worldwide. Garvey had over 6 million followers worldwide! This was before cell phones, internet and social media.

Garvey's incredible work reminds me of a lesson I learned while in Ghana. I was at a market looking to purchase some kente cloth for some clothes I wanted to have made. The brother selling the kente cloth said, "You should come to my village.

"Why?" I asked.

"I can get you any kind by of kente you want. I come from a village of weavers. *Every child in the village knows how to weave a full suite of clothes by the age of seven."*

This really had me think deeply. *What can our children produce by the age of 7...or 17 for that matter?!* I believe that if we were truly self-determined and self-sufficient the way we should be, every child, before graduating 8th grade would be able to:

- Make their own clothes
- Grow their own food
- Cook their own food
- Build a shelter/structure
- Defend themselves and their family

This should be the bare minimum if we ever expect to be a free and self-determining people. It is very doable if we have dedicated people who have a visionary consciousness of victory.

Delxino Wilson de Briano and his wife Deborah Wilson de Briano have picked up where Garvey left off. As the president and vice president of TAG TEAM Marketing, which produces **BuyBlackMovement.com** and the Black Business Network, they have built an organizational infrastructure which can take us to the achievements of Garvey and beyond.

BuyBlackMovement.com is a hub for Black businesses to market and distribute their products and services globally. Delxino and Debbie know a thing or two about marketing and distribution.

At the age of 23, they were broke, bankrupt, and living in a car with their college degrees. But by age 26, they were both millionaires. No…they did not sign a major sports or entertainment contract or win the lottery. They went into business. They made history as the most productive Black people in the history of network marketing. They built an organization of over 230,000 Black distributors serving over 3 million customers! They did all this however, in a White company. Their expertise made the company over $1 billion dollars in a twelve-year period. They only made just over $1 million for every $100 million they made the company.

They decided they could take their business-building knowledge and marketing expertise, and build something even bigger and better…and that's exactly what they did. **Today, in its infancy, BuyBlackMovement.com already has over 75,000 members in over 100 countries.** The Movement has also produced **MILLIONS IN SALES! Black people are buying Black!** Black companies in the network produce nutritional products, laundry detergent, soap, computers, games, jewelry, clothes, books, posters, and much, much more. **BuyBlackMovement.com** has re-directed millions of dollars back into the Black community to help these businesses thrive. This also creates more jobs and opportunities.

<u>**The reality is, no one is going to build Black business for Black people except Black people. If we work together, we can profit together.**</u> When Black people support Black businesses, we employ more of our own people, the economy of our communities thrive, and crime and violence decreases.

If you're going to bathe everyday anyway, why not switch to **one of the many Black-owned soap brands that BuyBlackMovement.com carries?** This is a lesson in leading by example, so others in our community will know that we can

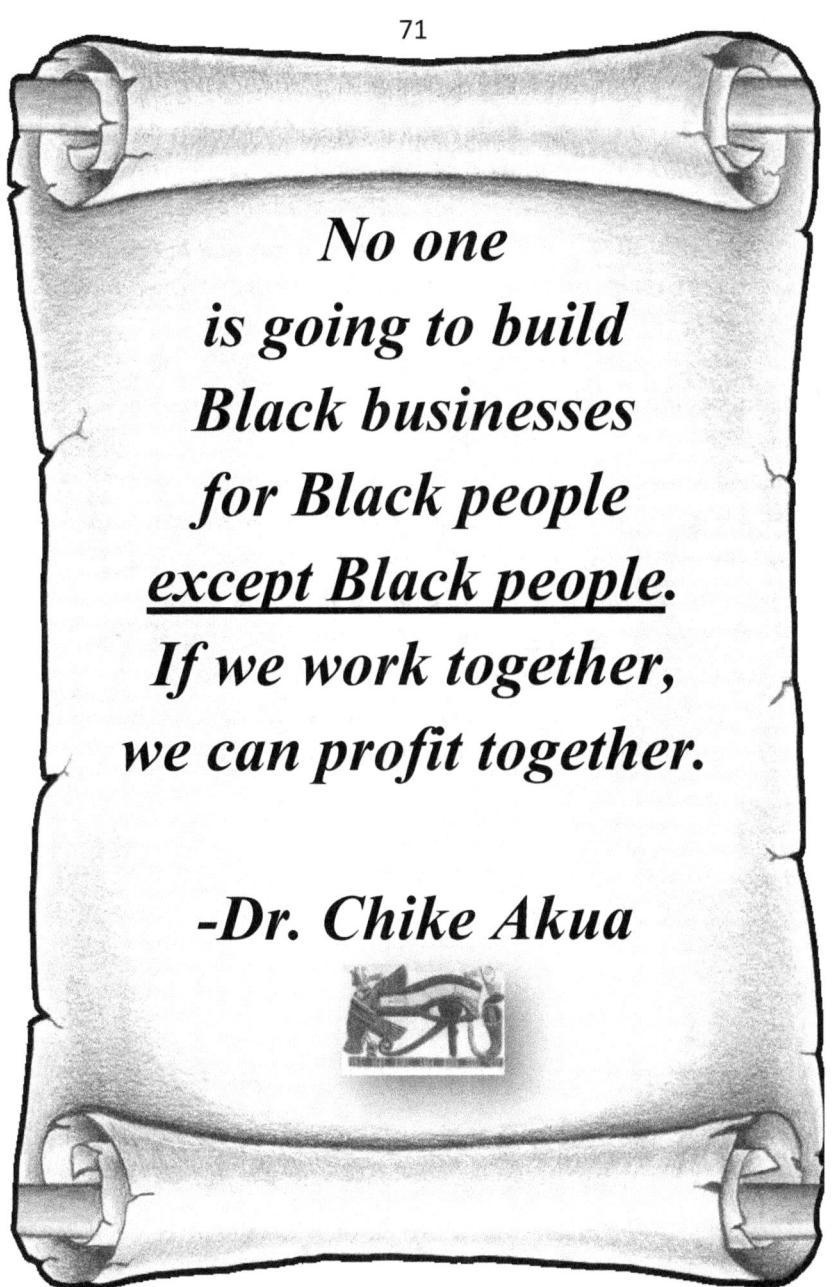

No one is going to build Black businesses for Black people <u>except Black people.</u> If we work together, we can profit together.

-Dr. Chike Akua

Chike Akua, Ph.D.

make and manufacture products just like anyone else can.

To fully participate from a position of power in the global economy, we must first maximize our own cultural economy. All other people participate in the global market place as a united group. So individual riches and personal prosperity mean nothing if they are not connected to collective wealth accumulation.

The Black Business Network is something you and your family should study and support. Every Black Family should be involved. They have periodic webcasts in which they conduct business training, cultural events, and conventions. *Many people talk about the need for Black economic development, but the Black Business Network is a proven system that everyone can participate and profit from.* Log on to **BuyBlackMovement.com/akua** to learn more about this essential movement for cooperative economics and wealth development. This is the kind of thinking and action it takes to help restore our people to their traditional greatness.

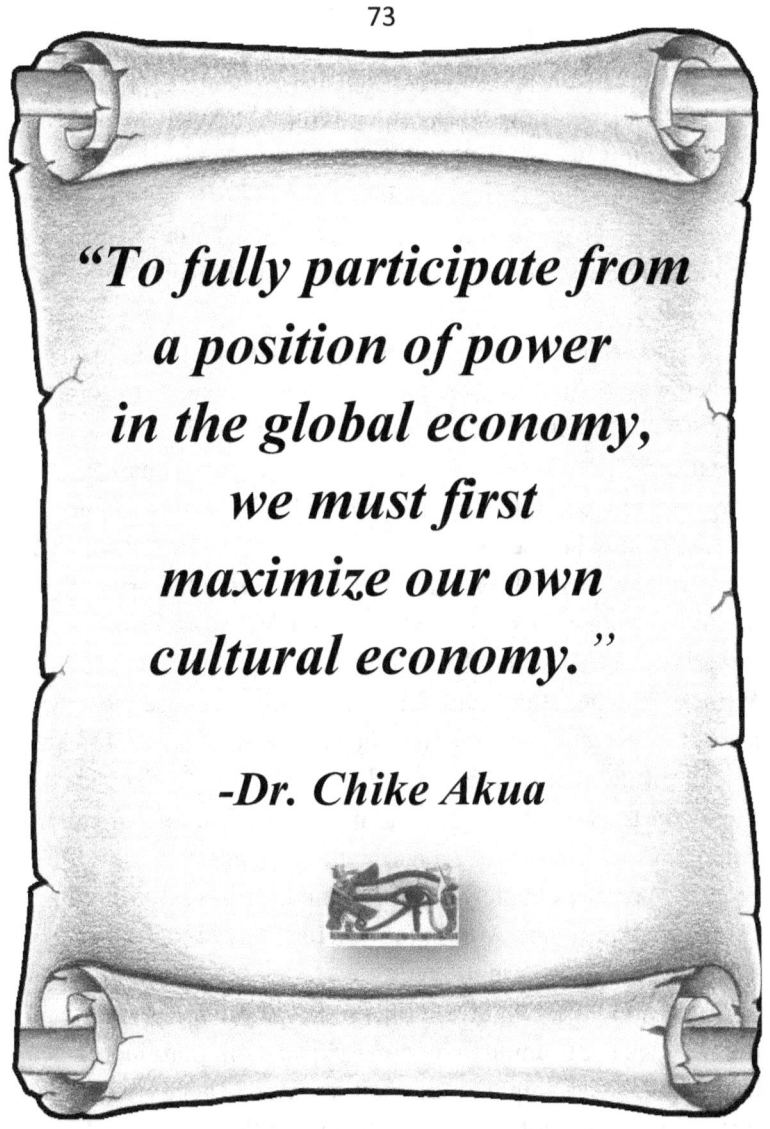

Learning & Practicing the Skill of Investing

College is a great time for learning, networking, and having fun. It is also a time when students should begin their journey to building their financial future. This is such a critical issue that by 2022, fourteen states passed legislation requiring financial literacy education as a requirement for high school graduation.

Learning to invest and trade in the stock market is a proven way to increase wealth and achieve financial freedom. The Stock Market has been called, *"The Great Wealth Equalizer."* Everyday people hear about the stock market, however, few people really understand how it works and how to "actively" buy and sell stocks.

However, African Americans, in particular, are not taking advantage of stocks. Statistics show that African Americans are 35% less likely to get involved in stocks as Whites. Another study said, "It's sad, really, because those who are not in the stock market are much poorer as a result. It's a big reason for the wealth gap." For these reasons, J.R. Fenwick founded FLipThatStock.com and it is the #1 site for African Americans to learn to invest and trade in stocks.

Average people work for money. But wealth-building people, in addition to working for money, have their money working for them through investing. Investing allows a person to own a small portion of a company (shares of stock) without the headaches of running a company (producing products, marketing, sales, shipping, accounting, etc). These are lessons that are typically not taught widely enough in the African American community.

Once you've been educated on the stock market, you can literally start investing and trading while in college! One of the best places to start investing is in the companies that produce the products you use every day along with the clothes and shoes you wear. Instead of just continuing to buy name-brand shoes, why not invest in the company that produces them?

As a student, YOU should learn:

1. What a stock is and how the stock market works
2. How to open an account to buy and sell stocks
3. How to find stocks to invest and trade
4. How to evaluate stocks
5. How to place an order to buy stocks
6. How to manage your risk and protect the money you've invested and are trading in stocks
7. How to track and monitor your stocks

If you know how to go online and shop for clothes, shoes and other goods, then you can learn how to invest. It really is just that easy. In the time it takes for you to read a social media post or make a social media post, you can place an order to invest in the stock(s) of your choice. It's that simple. And it doesn't take large amounts of money to get started. Learning to invest is a skill that every African American student should have and it's a skill that can literally pay for a lifetime. Go to FLipThatStock.com for a free video on "How to Get Started in the Stock Market."

Power & Political Participation

"How many marbles are in this jar?" "How many bubbles are in a bar of soap?" These are just a couple of the insidious kinds of questions Black people were asked by White polling officials when attempting to register to vote back in the 1950s and 60s. Tremendous measure were taken to see that Blacks did not exercise their constitutional right to vote.

About thirty years ago, as a young man, I was that brother who would say, *"I'm not into politics."* I would vote as a duty. But I was not politically aware or active. That is, until I heard a definition of politics that I could understand. I always thought of politics in terms of presidential politics and/or electoral politics. But politics is simply *the distribution of resources*. It refers to *who* gets *what, when, where* and *how much*. Politics determines who gets the new school in their community. It determines who gets the new community center, roads paved, garbage picked up, police protection, urban renewal grants to spur economic development and so much more.

The reason I had said, "I'm not into politics," is because I didn't recognize the relationship of politics to power. For African Americans, there has always been a stress on justice and power as it relates to politics. Karenga defined power as "a group's capacity to define, defend and develop its interests" (Karenga, 202, p. 360). Karenga defined politics as "the art and process of gaining, maintaining and using power" (Karenga, 2002, p. 350).

So I stopped saying I wasn't into politics when I realize *politics was into me every day*. I realized my tax dollars were either *directed into my community* or *diverted away from my community* based on my political participation. I realized all politics are local and local politics is the best place to start.

Because there have been so much corruption and scandals in the political sphere and because African Americans have been lied to and misused so much by politicians, it would be easy to be skeptical and cynical about politics. It's understandable. But nothing is gained from skepticism and cynicism. When we are organized as a collective with specific goals and aims, we can direct our economics and politics to produce profound results in the way of policies that empower us, monies allocated to our communities and resources allocated to meet our needs and solve our problems.

Voting does *not* solve all our problems, but it can lead to some solutions. If voting were not important, would Whites have passed laws preventing our ability to vote, then beat and lynched those who attempted to vote? Many would argue that we have an Ancestral Obligation to educate ourselves on the issues and vote. What do you think?

Below are four things you can do to:
1. Educate yourself on the issues.
2. Speak with other brothers and sisters on the issues to sharpen your position and to share with others.
3. If you are able, meet your local politicians, preferably with a group of like-minded brothers and sisters to share the needs of your community.
4. Vote and encourage members of your family, friends and community to vote.

Questions for Thought, Reflection & Discussion

1. Today, why is it impractical to simply say, "Go to school and get your education so you can get a good job?"
2. Did the 13th Amendment abolish slavery? Explain why or why not.
3. Explain why Marcus Garvey is a great example of Black economic empowerment? Who is continuing his work? Explain.
4. What must African Americans do to fully participate in the global economy?
5. Make a list of the top companies in America. How many of them are Black-owned?
6. Drive through your community and identify 10 Black-owned businesses. What products/services do they provide?
7. Log on to **BuyBlackMovement.com/akua** and create a FREE account. Watch the video clips on the front page and browse the wonderful products. Choose to receive two or three products per month by signing up as an Official Supporter.
8. Why should African Americans learn how to invest?
9. What is the difference between average people and wealth-building people?
10. What is the definition of politics?
11. What is the definition of power?
12. Why should African Americans be involved in the political process? Explain.

Step 4

Calling and Career Preparation

We have an Ancestral Obligation to operate out of a Higher Calling in service to our family, community and humanity.

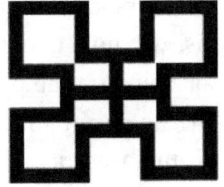

NSAA

"excellence and authenticity"

"He who does not know the real design will turn to an imitation."

Honoring Our Ancestral Obligations

As I have traveled the country conducting *SuccessQuest* for Students and *CareerQuest* Seminars, I have noticed that it is very important to define terms, especially those that are used loosely. Much attention is given in schools to supposedly preparing students for jobs and careers. What is a job? What is a career? A *job* is short-term work for the purpose of learning, earning and saving. Again, it is short-term. A *career* is an occupation or profession requiring specialized training. A career is long-term.

Oftentimes, we see people bouncing from job to job because they never established a *career*. But we can also take this a step further. Jobs and careers are critical, but to truly Honor Our Ancestral Obligations, we must understand our *calling*. A calling is your purpose for being on the planet; it is your reason for being. Traditional African spirituality (and many other religious, cultural and spiritual traditions) tells us that all of us have been sent here for a powerful and particular purpose. Traditional African systems of education were aimed at helping one understand the nature of their calling and then equipping them with skills to execute and live their calling with character, consciousness and commitment.

The cultural, economic and technological landscape of America and the world has shifted tremendously over the past 20-30 years. Jobs and careers that were once abundant no longer exist. New careers and opportunities for economic growth and opportunity have emerged. This, coupled with the fact that today, far too many people do not know their purpose for being on the planet, has caused tremendous problems in the Black community. In addition, visual media and social media provide *weapons of mass deception, weapons of mass distraction*, and *weapons of mass destruction* to successfully keep many from knowing that they have a higher calling. This, then, keeps them from pursuing it. Technology and media are tools that can be used to truly transform lives when properly used. But far too often they are used inappropriately and with improper priority.

The results of large numbers of purposeless people in our communities has been devastating. *If you don't know your purpose, others will assign you a purpose.* So if you don't know your purpose--*great*--society assigns young Black males the purpose of making money for them as an inmate doing slave labor. When a young Black female doesn't know her purpose, this society assigns her the purpose of being an object of sexual pleasure and manipulation. If you don't know your purpose, others will assign you a purpose—and you may not like the purpose others have for you. **You have an Ancestral Obligation to find and live your Divine purpose.**

Anyone who wants to be successful in today's society must be very wise in their pursuit of knowledge, skills, education and a higher calling. There are several keys that will assist you in finding your calling and establishing a successful career. The first is vision. **Vision** *is the ability to see beyond your circumstances. It is a picture of the possibilities, a snapshot of your success.* If there's something you don't like about your life, your family, your community, you can envision something more empowering—then create it. We are in many ways the products of our own visions. But if we lack vision, we become increasingly vulnerable to all of the ills of society. There are three types of vision you should be aware of:

> *"Vision is the ability to see beyond your circumstances."*
>
> -Dr. Chike Akua

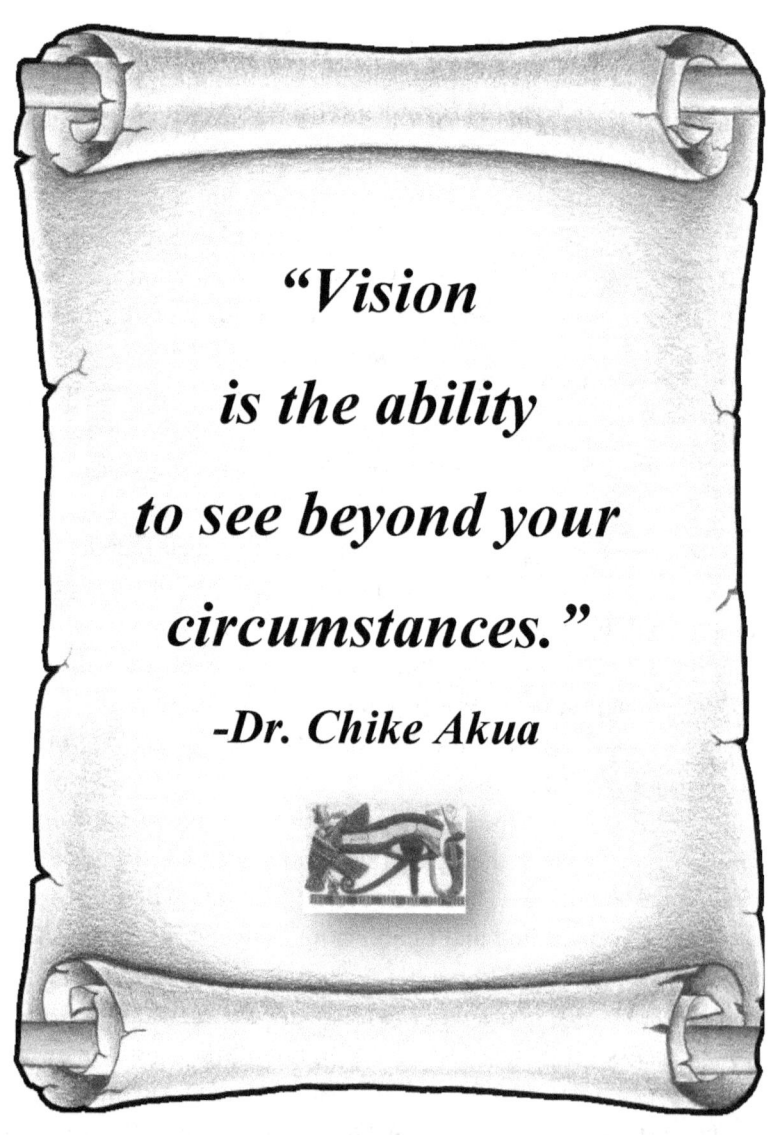

1. **Hindsight**: It has been said that "hindsight is 20/20 (perfect) vision." That means, if you had known what you know now, you wouldn't have made the mistakes that you have made. Hindsight, in the literal sense, is the ability to see what's behind you. But figuratively speaking, hindsight is studying and seeing extraordinary people and patterns of excellence they produced. This is essential so you can avoid their mistakes and reproduce and build upon their successes. This is one of the reasons *why there is an African Proverb which says, "To return to the past is the first step forward."* To know where you're going, you must first know where you and your people have been.

2. **Insight**: An essential aspect of traditional African systems of education was the cultivation of inner vision or insight. Insight can be defined as gaining knowledge of the nature or inner workings of someone or something. Insight into the inner workings of life, success and empowerment requires that we reduce the volume of outside noises and distractions and take time each day to be quiet with ourselves. There is an ancient Scripture that says, "Be still and know that I am God." It is in the stillness that insights emerge. And there are certain high-level insights that are available only to those who set aside sacred time each day for the practice of meditation, reflection, and prayer.

3. **Foresight**: The ability to see patterns, events, trends and innovative ideas before they become manifest in the visible world is called foresight. Some people are gifted with this ability. However, the skill can be cultivated with focus and discipline. Again, our traditional systems of education prepared students to be able to access these powers. As with anything else, the more the skills are practiced, one gains tremendous, seemingly other-worldly abilities to see things before they happen.

As you gain a deeper understanding of the three kinds of vision, be mindful that you must practice envisioning every day. It is best to have a set time of the day in the morning and evening to do this. *When you first wake up and just before going to sleep are critical times when the mind is most susceptible to suggestion. You can, through envisioning, make a virtual visitation to the place of empowerment in life you are seeking. You can and must control and direct your visions.* Your visions should be clear, conscious, convincing and compelling. Your visions must be vivid, not vague. Envision with precision. Let it be colorful and detailed. Let there be no limits or boundaries to your visions. Your visions should serve the greatest good for your family, community and humanity.

Once you have begun to cultivate the ability to envision, you will also need valor. **Valor** is the courage to step out on faith and bring your vision to reality. There will be opposition to your visions, so only share your visions with people of like minds and spirit. Surround yourself with people who are looking for more in life and who can handle expansive visions.

Before you set off to make your visions a reality, be very clear about your values. **Values** are the principles, beliefs and morals that you use to guide your life, your thoughts, words and actions. Your vision must be aligned to your values because there will be all sorts of "opportunities" offered to you that are not aligned with your values. In addition, you must constantly re-evaluate your values to make sure they are consistent with the best tradition of our Ancestors.

Now that you are examining your calling and envisioning a powerful, prosperous and productive future, you will need to be aware of options for your continuing education.

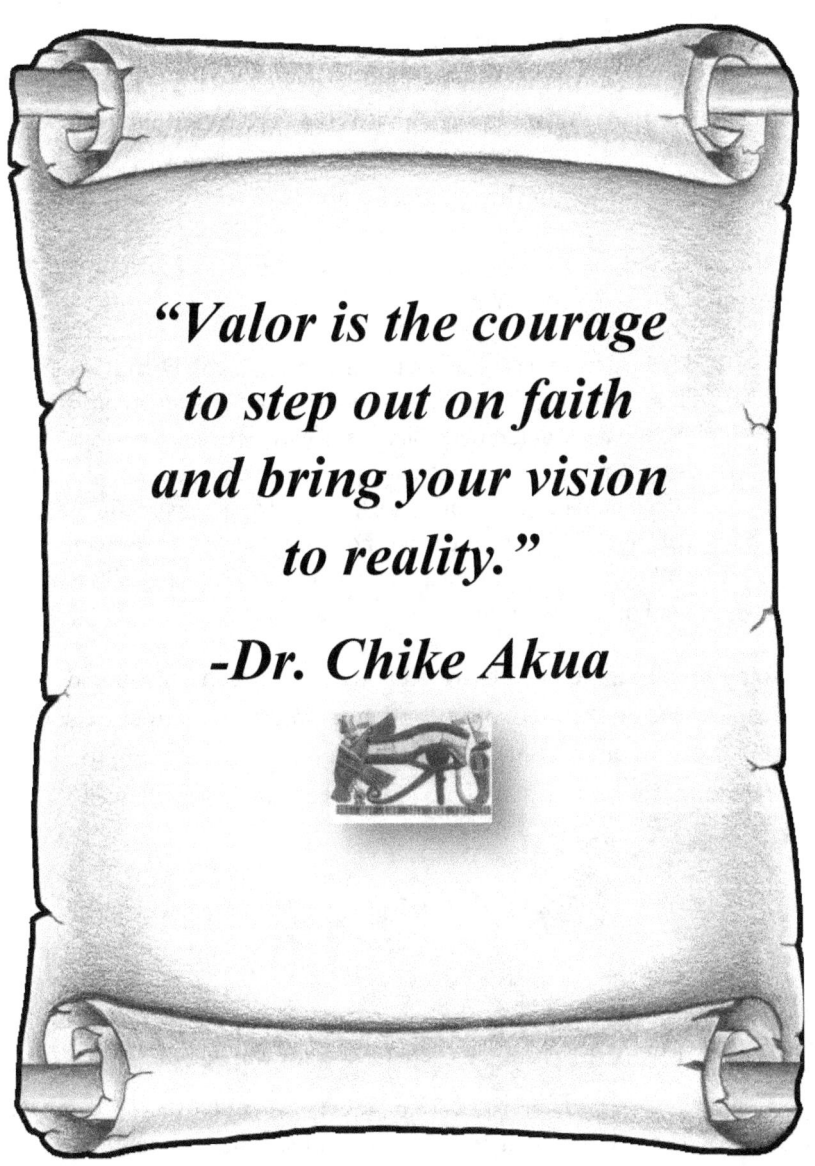

"Valor is the courage to step out on faith and bring your vision to reality."

-Dr. Chike Akua

As indicated earlier, there has been a shift in terms of viable options available to youth in today's economy. This is not necessarily bad, it just requires a different type of preparation. Unfortunately, many schools are way behind in terms of preparing students for the practical realities of today's world.

Consider this example that Dr. Jawanza Kunjufu gives in his book *Black Economics*:

> "It used to be that an African American male in Detroit could drop out of high school in his junior year and work in one of the big three automobile plants and earn between $10-15 an hour, and because of a strong union, he would receive adequate medical benefits, vacation and a lucrative retirement package. The above scenario no longer exists for teenagers still dropping out in great numbers in many cities to earn that kind of money (Kunjufu, 1992, p. 83).

Many jobs like the one described above have been outsourced overseas or, due to technology and automation, no longer exist. This means a new set of skills are needed and while going to college is a good thing, college is not necessarily the answer.

Whatever profession or career you decide to pursue, consider a career in one of the STEM fields. STEM stands for Science, Technology, Engineering and Mathematics. There are some states that use the acronym STEAM. The "A" may refer to Agriculture or the Arts. While Black people introduced the world to the STEM and STEAM fields and achieved mightily in them, there is now an underrepresentation of Black people and people of color in these fields. It is now clear that America cannot advance itself (once again) without the expertise of Blacks in these fields. But you should pursue them as a part of your Ancestral Obligation. Do your "due diligence" (research) to determine which of these may be best for you.

There is an African Proverb which says, "When the music changes, so does the dance." This means that one must learn to adjust to changes they cannot control. Far too many people are graduating with bachelor's degrees, masters degrees and even Ph.D's only to find that there are not enough jobs available for their chosen field. Not only this, but the disappointment is further compounded when one realizes they have tens of thousands of dollars to pay back in student loans and now must figure out how to make ends meet. So more and more people are coming to question the practicality of a college degree. This is not to discourage one from getting a college education. It is to say that the degree itself it not enough. There are skills you must have along with the degree.

According to George Fraser, author of *Success Runs in Our Race* and *Race for Success*, networking and high-level interpersonal skills will set you apart from others in a powerful and meaningful way. Your ability to build rapport and cultivate relationships makes all the difference in acquiring jobs, promotions, critical information and contracts for services.

"*When the music changes, so does the dance.*"
-African Proverb

To Honor Our Ancestral Obligations, we must understand that education is a must from the cradle to the grave. As mentioned before, Dr. Carter G. Woodson, in his powerful book, *The Mis-education of the Negro*, notes that ***there are two kinds of education: the kind you are given and the kind you must give yourself (Woodson, 1933). There are a number of valuable skills that you can teach yourself that don't necessarily require a college degree:***

- Video editing
- Audio engineering
- Website design
- Computer coding
- Computer service (debugging, virus protection, software installation)
- Social media marketing
- Landscaping
- Agricultural engineering (growing food)
- Basic auto mechanics

In addition, there are certain occupations that require specialized training where one can earn just as much or more in terms of income than a college graduate. Training in the areas of:

- HVAC (heating and air conditioning)
- Welding
- Auto mechanics
- Barbering and cosmetology
- Construction, plumbing, music and video production

Many of the programs which certify people in these areas often only require two years or less of schooling. In addition, the programs offer "on-the-job" training. In the new economy, students should have at least one specific, marketable skill such as some of those listed above.

There is, quite regrettably, a phenomenon that stops many Black youth dead in their tracks from pursuing their calling and career. It is here that we must discuss some ways to prevent the continuation of mass Black incarceration.

Countering Mass Incarceration

"SIR, WHY DID YOU BLOCK TRAFFIC? WHAT WERE YOU THINKING PULLING THAT TRUCK OUT AND BLOCKING TRAFFIC LIKE THAT? DO YOU KNOW THAT'S AGAINST THE LAW?!" The white officer shouted in my face as he continued with question after question. A flash of heat and angry energy streaked through my body.

"Are you going to let me answer you?" I asked calmly but firmly.

He paused briefly.

I was 26 years old. My wife and I were moving from Virginia to Georgia. I had rented a large truck and hitched my car on the back. My wife was driving in front of me, leading the way in her car. We had just left the house and I was about to pull onto a major thoroughfare. After waiting almost five minutes, I pulled out into traffic and blocked one side of the north-bound traffic, until the south-bound side cleared so I could turn. Clearly this was unlawful, but clearly the officer's angry and confrontational approach was unnecessary. He seemed like he was my age or younger. He was small in stature and really seemed like he had something to prove. He went on with a barrage of questions yelling and pointing at me while walking closer. I had to quickly and carefully calm myself down knowing that this could escalate into a volatile confrontation.

In the meantime, my wife, seeing that I had been pulled over, doubled back around and pulled over in front of the truck I was driving. She got out of the car to see what was going on.

"MA'AM GET BACK IN YOUR CAR—NOW!" shouted the officer.

"Oh hellllll nooo!" I thought to myself. "Nobody talks to my wife like that!" But I had to keep that inside, because that response would have taken this encounter to a place I was not prepared to go. I was prepared to go to Georgia, not to jail. I wanted to say, **"Who the #@& do you think you're talking to?!"** But that was not the tactically wise thing to do. The officer turned back toward me, forcefully repeating his original question.

"Sir, I was waiting to pull into traffic for about five minutes," I explained calmly but firmly. "Each time there was only a break in traffic on one side but not the other. So I pulled out halfway until the other side cleared. I'm moving with my wife to Georgia."

I don't know why they rent you guys these huge trucks when you have no experience driving them!" he said, still in an aggravated tone, but clearly calming down. After taking my license and registration and checking it, he said in the same aggravated tone, "I don't want to see this happen again!"

"Sir, like I said, I'm moving to Georgia. As soon as you give me my license and registration, you will never see me again." He handed me my license and registration and we departed.

Like many other Black men, I have had several undesirable encounters with the police. I can say, without a doubt, if I had not been very strategic in how I handled each situation, it is most likely that I would be dead or in prison. The above situation could have turned out very differently if I had allowed my ego to get in the way. That officer seemed like he was looking for a reason to pull his gun or lock someone up.

Police have a very difficult job. I salute those officers of all ethnicities that take their job to "protect and serve" seriously. There have been times when I hated to see an officer coming and other times when I was relieved to see an officer coming. I know Black police officers who became law enforcement officers because they saw how their own people were often treated and that there was a lack of Blacks in law enforcement. *In the 1960s, groups like the Deacons for Defense, the Black Panthers and others recognized the police as an army of occupation that consistently terrorized Black communities. These groups organized themselves to protect the Black community from rogue cops who made beating, shooting and killing Blacks almost like a sport for fun.*

XIIIIXIIIIXIIIIXIII   Chike Akua, Ph.D.   **XIIIIXIIIIXIIIIXIII**

Honoring Our Ancestral Obligations

I salute the courageous Blacks who armed and organized themselves to protect our communities. I also salute the courageous souls who confronted law enforcement during various demonstrations around the country in response to police brutality and murders. We must continue to organize and resist police brutality.

There is an African Proverb which says, "Strategy is better than strength." No education of Black people would be complete without clear insights and instructions about how to handle ourselves in the presence of law enforcement. *Like chess, every move counts and you have to think several steps ahead or you'll be put in check mate!*

The racial reckoning of the summer of 2020 after the murder of George Floyd, Brianna Taylor and Ahmaud Arbury along with the previous well-known murders of Trayvon Martin (Sanford, FL), Eric Garner (NY), Mike Brown (Ferguson, MO), Tamir Rice (Cleveland, OH), Walter Scott (North Charleston, SC) and Sandra Bland (Hempstead, TX) have brought the nation's attention to a problem that has been pervasive for as long as the United States of America has existed. We extend condolences to the families of those who have lost a loved one to terrorism and police brutality.

"Strategy is better than strength."

-African Proverb

It should be noted that there has not necessarily been an escalation in these kinds of acts. It is simply that, with technology, now, more examples of police brutality are being captured on cell phones and shared quickly, going viral on social media. *Had Black people not placed these stories in broad circulation via social media, the national media outlets never would have. Make no mistake about it, it is clear—Black people are under siege by police.* A whole separate volume on how we need to organize to police and protect our people in our communities is much needed, but that is not the purpose of this particular discourse. *The purpose of this conversation is for you to understand how to handle yourself as an individual in a potentially volatile situation. How we handle ourselves in situations with law enforcement can escalate or de-escalate a situation quickly. Split seconds count, personal and discipline and mental mastery will make all the difference.*

As a prerequisite, it is wise not to be in the company of friends and acquaintances who are loud and obnoxious in public. It could be harmless fun to you, however, tactically, it is very foolish. A moment of foolishness can end in a lifetime of pain, for you and those you love. First, this dishonors our Ancestors, Elders and our whole culture. It is simply foolish and puts your ignorance on display for the world to see. Never mind the fact that *White youth can and do get away with many things Black youth cannot get away with*. For the purposes of this discussion, focusing on that would take us from our immediate objective—your safety. Second, this draws unnecessary attention to the group and places you in a position to be confronted by authorities. I am quite aware that just being Black and in a group is enough to be confronted by

"Do not quarrel with a leopard if you have no spear."
-African Proverb

authorities, however, we are not referring to such situations at this particular time.

Any war is made up of many battles and sometimes one must surrender a battle to win a war. In my personal opinion, a traffic stop or encounter with the police is not the time or place to show how big and bad you are or to educate a law enforcement officer on how they are violating your constitutional rights or participating in the system of racism and white supremacy ideology. ***There is an African Proverb which says, "A wise man fills his brain before emptying his mouth."*** Because I know Black males are under siege, I am not going to empty my mouth with words to antagonize and upset an officer who may already be bent on my destruction. ***There is also an African Proverb which says, "Do not quarrel with a leopard if you have no spear."***

The following are steps I have taken that have proven very helpful, however, it should be noted that because there are some sick officers on the streets this may not always work, given that we are in a racist society. Nonetheless, here are a few steps that I strongly advise:

1. **Remain calm and centered.** Your disposition, the spirit and energy you bring to the situation, can and often does determine the outcome of a situation.
2. **In addressing a law enforcement officer, always be respectful.** Officers want to be respected like anyone else. Speaking respectfully can immediately make an officer less guarded, fearful or agitated. Many acts of police brutality are caused by an officer who is fearful of Black males or Black people.

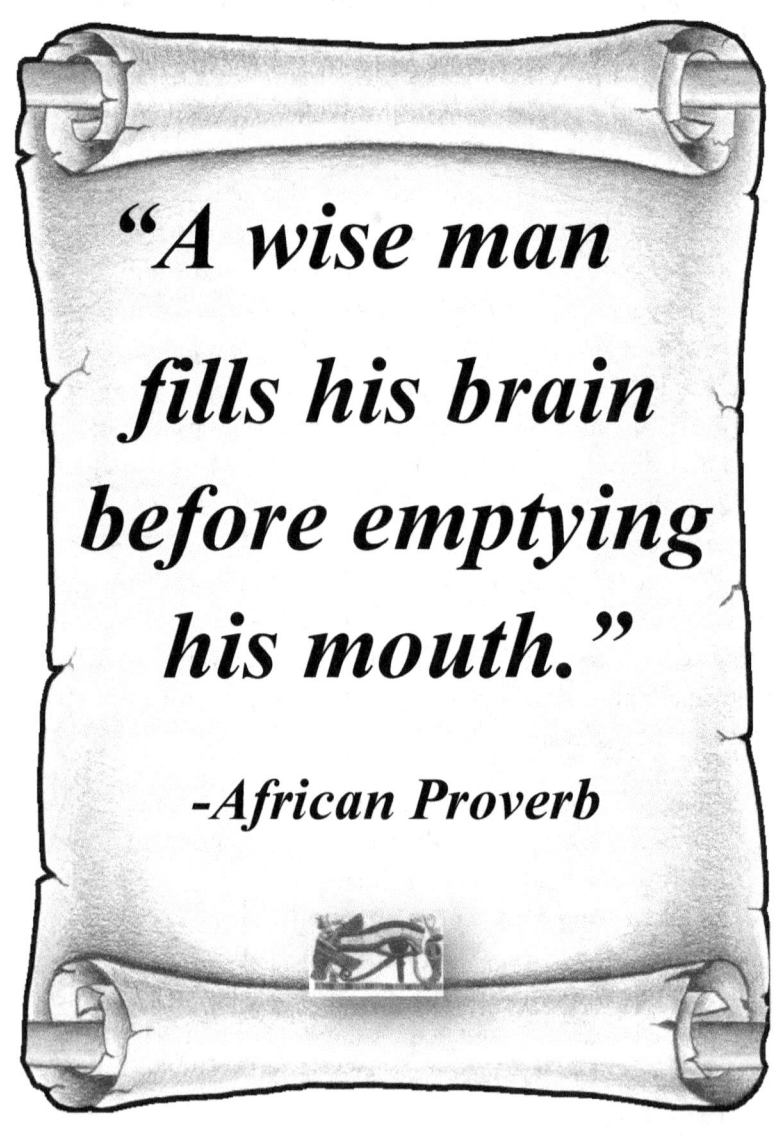

"*A wise man fills his brain before emptying his mouth.*"

-African Proverb

3. **Keep your hands visible at all times. If pulled over for a traffic stop, keep both hands on the steering wheel.** It is important for the officer to know that you are unarmed. If on the streets, keep your hands in front of you and out of your pockets.
4. **Make no sudden moves.** Announce what you are about to do or ask permission: "May I go in the glove compartment to get my car registration?"
5. **Follow instructions as they are given and when they are given.** Do everything the officer says that is within reason and within the law.

Again, I am well aware that the above steps are not 100% fail safe. I am aware that you could do all of the above and still be victimized. But these are basic steps you can take to at least give you the best chance of getting home safely. In *The New Jim Crow*, Michelle Alexander has thoroughly documented the inequities of mass incarceration and money-making manipulation in the prison industrial complex of America. We don't need you to be the next hashtag for being arrested and becoming a victim of the system.

Questions for Thought, Reflection & Discussion

1. Explain the difference between a job and a career.
2. Explain the difference between a career and a calling.
3. Define the following terms:
   a. vision
   b. hindsight
   c. insight
   d. foresight
   e. valor
   f. values
4. There is an African Proverb which says, "When the music changes, so does the dance." Explain what this means in relation to the current economic landscape and how one must choose his/her career.
5. List some valuable skills you can use to make money that do not require a college education? Which, if any, appeal to you?
6. Share your opinion about this statement and how it relates to communicating with law enforcement: "Sometimes you must give up a battle to be around to win the war."
7. Explain the following African Proverbs:
   a. "Strategy is better than strength."
   b. "A wise man fills his head before opening his mouth."
   c. "Do not quarrel with a leopard if you have no spear."

Step 5

Spiritual Transformation:

The Eternal & Essential Energy That That Gives & Guides

We have an Ancestral Obligation to be spirit-centered in all we do.

GYE NYAME
"Omnipotence of God"

As a junior English major in college, I had to take an advanced writing course. For our final project, the professor said we must choose a magazine and submit an article for publication. One evening, while in my dorm room working on the assignment, I had a transformational experience. This was at a time when my cultural and spiritual consciousness was really expanding. The subject of my article was about how Black men were constantly being referred to in the national media as an *endangered species*—a designation usually reserved for animals. Reading through all of the literature was depressing and would make you think we didn't have a chance as a people.

I wanted to write something positive and uplifting about great Black men that are usually not talked about. As I sat at my desk brainstorming, in front of me was a postcard-size picture of Frederick Douglass and Martin Luther King. I was suddenly struck by a presence in my room. It was so strong it knocked me to my knees. It was clear to me that this presence was the Spirit of my Creator.

I knelt down next to my bed to pray, which I had not done since I was six years old. I asked for guidance, because the challenges facing our people seemed overwhelming. The response to my prayer was that I could not do anything for my people without the help of the Creator; but *with* the help of the Creator, I could accomplish anything I wished. I humbly asked forgiveness for my faults and failings and asked for the Creator's assistance in helping to resurrect African people. After the prayer, I felt a release as if a weight had been lifted from my shoulders. I felt empowered and emboldened to take on the mission of being a messenger.

I dedicated myself to prayer, going to church, studying the Bible, the teachings of Yeshua (Jesus) and reading books about African history and culture. I went through a traditional

African Rites of Passage Program on campus which further developed my discipline, my sense of purpose and my cultural and spiritual consciousness. When the elder brothers in the Rites of Passage examined my character, I was given the name *Chike*, which, in the Ibo nation (present-day Nigeria) means, "Power of God." From that day to this, I have been on a mission. My transformation happened at the age of twenty-one. But far too many brothers and sisters have already made negative, life-altering decisions by that age that are very difficult to recover from. Your spiritual transformation cannot wait another day.

One of the original names of Africa was *Alkebulan*. It means, "Land of the Spirit People." This is because African people have always been a deeply spiritual people. We have always believed in and served One Supreme Being, known by many names and worshiped in many ways. We have always given praises to the Most High. Spirit was an everyday part of every aspect of our lives. We brought spirit to science, spirit to mathematics, spirit to reading, writing, language, literature, agriculture, astronomy and every aspect of life and living.

Asa Hilliard tells us that ancient Africans arrived at their belief in One Supreme Being through science (Hilliard, 1995). Through the meticulous observation of natural phenomena, it

> *"Spirituality is the recognition and respect for the eternal and essential energy that gives and guides us in all things."*
> *—Dr. Chike Akua*

became clear that there was a Supreme Intelligence guiding everything. They noticed that the sun rises in the east and sets in the west. They noticed that the moon went through phases every 28 days. They noticed the cycles of high tide and low tide. They noticed the appearance of certain stars and constellations and their procession across the sky over the course of each month and each year. All of these cycles and processes pointed to the reality of a Universal Architect, a spirit and energy that was in and around everyone and everything.

But we live in a society that attempts to *de-spiritualize* everything. Spirit has been removed from the education process, from the healing process, and from the birthing and child-rearing process. The enslavement process attempted to make us think that all things African were evil and ungodly. In the African worldview (perspective), it is unthinkable to speak of things as critical as raising children, education, sex, healing, family, and one's life purpose and not bring a discussion of spirit and spirituality into the process. So, what is spirituality?

We are told in western civilization that there is a separation between church and state, and a separation between the spiritual and the material. In the African worldview, and many other indigenous cultures, nothing could be further from the truth. There can be no material object or life without the spiritual giving it the power to exist. This eternal energy is the One Source and the One Force through which we live, move, and have our being. It is both immanent (within us) and transcendent (around and above us).

Spirituality could be described as the recognition and respect for the eternal and essential energy that gives and guides us in all things. It is our relationship to this spirit and energy that we should surrender to. We are deeply spiritual beings who come to this reality connected to the spirit realm.

However, many schools and society, in general, attempt to stifle the spirit of the children, because they do not know how to properly nourish and nurture the spirit of the child. If you are not spiritually-centered, you may end up unconsciously doing the same thing.

This discussion should not be confused with religion. Religion is man-made. Spirituality is God-given. Religion is man's best and worst attempt to know God. I say "man's" attempt, because, often, in western religions, women were left out of the process and were oppressed *by* the process. One's religion can assist in developing their spirituality or it can hinder the process. So this territory must be navigated carefully and prayerfully.

The following are seven things you should know about the African-centered understanding of Spirit.

Seven Observations About Spirit

1. Spirit is the One Source and the One Force through which we live, move, and have our being.
2. Spirit is known by many names and worshiped in many ways.
3. Spirit is both immanent (within us) and transcendent (around and above us).
4. Spirit is the activating energy and original essence that causes all things to occur.
5. Spirit moves in the midst of everything we do.

6. When we get in touch and in tune with Spirit, we can use it to guide our thoughts, words, and actions and shape our life and reality.
7. Spirit is much like the wind in that it is difficult to find its origin or destination, but we can harness it and ride the current when we recognize its patterns.

African people developed many ways of engaging with Spirit. Spiritual disciplines were embedded and woven into the fabric of their system of education and socialization. For example, in ancient Kemet, people were to live by the **Seven Principles of Ma'at.** Below is the list and a brief explanation of each principle:

1. <u>Truth</u>-that which is based in honesty and integrity
2. <u>Justice</u>-fairness in all things
3. <u>Righteousness</u>-right thoughts, words, and deeds
4. <u>Reciprocity</u>-what goes around comes around
5. <u>Balance</u>-giving appropriate attention and energy to what is important
6. <u>Order</u> – all things are done decently and in a proper fashion
7. <u>Harmony</u>-living peacefully with all things (Hilliard, 1995).

It was said that the Creator used these principles to shape, fashion, and form the Universe and that humans must live according to these principles in order to live an abundant life. The ancient Book of Khunanup declares, "The balancing of the land is in Ma'at" (Karenga, 1984, p. 32). As we are balanced *internally*, we will see our reality balanced *externally*. This takes tremendous *intention* and *attention* to the things of the Spirit. So important was Ma'at as a spiritual principle of governance that

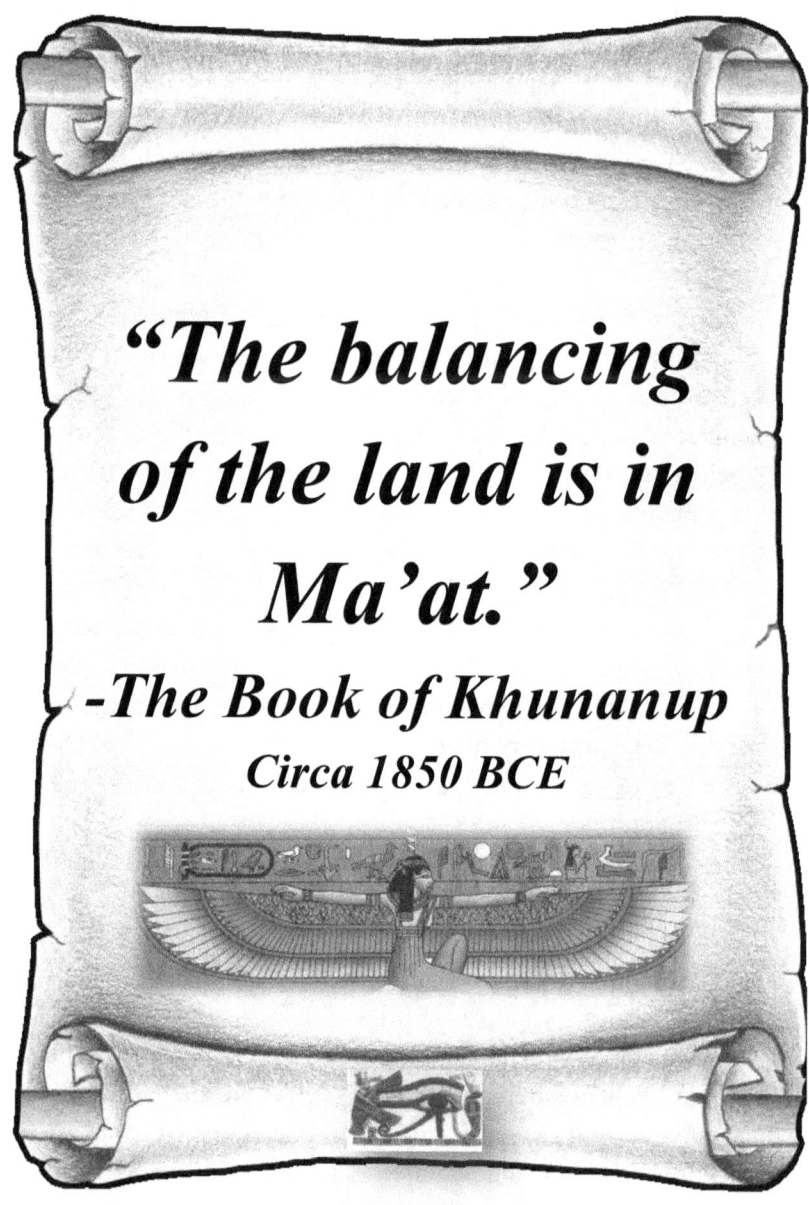

"The balancing of the land is in Ma'at."
-*The Book of Khunanup*
Circa 1850 BCE

XIIIIXIIIIXIIIIXIII   Chike Akua, Ph.D.   XIIIIXIIIIXIIIIXIII

Ma'at was pictured as an African woman with wings and a feather in her headband. The wings represented the ability to fly high above life's challenges from living a life of virtue (truth, justice and righteousness). The feather in her headband represented having a heart that is lighter than a feather. Being able to balance the Scales of Ma'at became the goal of life.

It was believed that, upon death, your heart was symbolically placed on one side of the Scale and a feather was placed on the other side of the Scale. If your heart was not weighed down with wrong thoughts, wrong words and wrong actions, then your heart was as light as a feather and you were able to balance the Scales of Ma'at. You were declared to be **"Ma'at Kheru" or "True of Voice."**

In West Africa, it was understood that human beings had a reason for being sent here to earth. The *Odu Ifa*, the ethical and spiritual teaching of the Yoruba people says, "Surely humans were chosen to bring good into the world" (Karenga, 1999, p. 228). This gives every human being a purpose and a mission. This, then, must be the mission and purpose we pass on to our children. *We must choose our life's work based on our life's mission and purpose. This is how we will be fulfilled because our work will be a labor of love.* Again, the ancient sage and Scribe, Dja Ptahhotep, observed, "Love for the work they do brings people closer to God" (Hilliard, 1987, p. 28)

The Seven Principles of Kwanzaa

In 1966, after many years of community activism, Maulana Karenga realized that one of most critical challenges facing Black people was that we did not have a Black value system. So, after studying a number of traditional African customs, traditions and values, he created Kwanzaa. Kwanzaa is a Swahili word which means "first fruits." It refers to a time of

> *"Surely humans have been chosen to bring good into the world."*
>
> *-Odu Ifa*
> The Ethical & Spiritual Teachings of the Yoruba

year when African people would gather to give thanks and praises to the Creator, honor to the Ancestors, and celebrate a bountiful harvest and all that is good.

While Kwanzaa is an annual African American cultural celebration that takes place from December 26-January 1, it's principles are meant to be practiced throughout the year.

In creating Kwanzaa, Dr. Karenga codified (brought together) the principles that have sustained our power as a people for millennia. These principles are called the *Nguzo Saba* (Seven Principles). All the principles are in the language of Swahili. *While Kwanzaa is not a religious holiday, you will notice a spiritual thread that runs through each of the principles:*

Nguzo Saba (Seven Principles)

1. **Umoja** (Unity): to strive for and maintain unity in the family, community, nation, and race.
2. **Kujichagulia** (Self-determination): to define ourselves, name ourselves, create for ourselves, and speak for ourselves.
3. **Ujima** (Collective Work & Responsibility): to build and maintain our community together and to make our brothers' and sisters' problems our problems and to solve them together.
4. **Ujamaa** (Cooperative Economics): to build and maintain our own stores, shops, and other businesses and to profit from them together.
5. **Nia** (Purpose): to make as our collective vocation the building and developing of our community in order to restore our people to their traditional greatness.

6. **Kuumba** (Creativity): to do always as much as we can in the way we can, in order to leave our community more beautiful and beneficial than we inherited it.
7. **Imani** (Faith): To believe with all our heart in our people, our parents, our teachers, our leaders and the righteousness and victory of our struggle (Karenga, 1998, p. 7-8).

As you consider these observations about spirit and values, below are some ways you can continue to elevate, celebrate, and cultivate spiritual understandings and awakenings in yourself and others.

Seven Ways to Cultivate Spiritual Power

1. Commit *yourself* to reading, learning, and living a spirit-centered life.
2. Spend time in nature. Ghanaian mystic, Ishmael Tetta, says, "Nature is the autobiography of God."
3. Listen more closely and attentively to what your intuition tells you.
4. Become a part of a faith-based community (church, mosque, temple), especially one that has effective programs for young people.
5. Set aside a quiet time every day (5-15 minutes) to read and reflect on a brief Scripture. Deep breathing and meditation during this time can also have profound long-term health and behavioral benefits.
6. Share and celebrate the **Seven Principles of Kwanzaa** and the **Seven Principles of Ma'at** year round. Make the understanding and practice of these principles a part of your everyday life.

> *"Love for the work they do brings people closer to God."*
>
> -Dja Ptahhotep
> *Ancient Sage & Scribe of Kemet*

7. Everyone is sent to this time, place, and space for a powerful purpose and a mighty mission. Examine your gifts, talents, and abilities in order to arrive at your life's purpose. Determine to live out your higher purpose.

Questions for Thought, Reflection & Discussion

1. How did ancient Africans arrive at their belief in a Supreme Being?
2. Of the Seven Observations About Spirit, which one stands out to you? Explain why.
3. Of the Seven Principles of Ma'at, which one stands out to you? Explain why.
4. Of the Seven Principles of Kwanzaa, which one stands out to you? Explain why. Which do you think you can apply to your personal life right away?
5. What is most significant about the spiritual or religious instruction you have received thus far in your life? Explain.

Step 6

Relationship Revolution & Family Restoration

We have an Ancestral Obligation to revitalize our relationships and restore our families.

AYA
"endurance"

Honoring Our Ancestral Obligations

I am the last of five children. As such, I was born into a family system in which rules, roles, and responsibilities were clearly defined and already known for the most part. So I fell right in. These rules, roles and responsibilities were reinforced constantly through verbal reminders, chores, rewards and punishments. My parents worked hard to provide a stable environment and rich cultural experiences. *What kind of family did you grow up in? What would you like your family to be like ten years from now?*

My mother grew up without the love of a father—he died when she was an infant. My father grew up without the love of a mother—she died when he was a young boy. It is as if both of my parents made an ***internal affirmation*** that they would build a strong family so that their children could have what they did not. While our family had its fair share of problems, we were truly blessed because of my parents' commitment.

We have an Ancestral Obligation to carefully examine the construction of our family, revitalize relationships and restore family. And it is here that we must make an internal affirmation that we will build and develop strong families. This affirmation brings with it the realization that careful consideration must be given to career trajectory, financial habits, dating/courting, sexual activity, and much, much more.

Family is the cornerstone of a community and the foundation of great nations and civilizations. It is in the family that we learn what to value, how to work, our larger purpose, guiding beliefs, cherished traditions, spirituality, loving relationships and much, much more. In *They Stole It But You Must Return It*, Richard Williams tells us:

> A man without his family is like a lion without his teeth; he has the heart and the power, but he cannot overcome his prey. A woman without her family is like a bird with

"*Family is the cornerstone of a community and the foundation of great nations and civilizations.*"

-Dr. Chike Akua

a broken wing; her ability to fly is inhibited. And worse yet, a child without his family is like a ship caught on a rough sea without a rudder" (Williams, 2010, p. 7).

The Black family was under siege the moment Europeans invaded Africa over 500 years ago…and it is still under siege today. In addition, we were never provided reparations to repair the damage that was done. It is not by chance that over 70% of Black children are born to unwed mothers and that over 1 million black men are in prison. These facts notwithstanding, *you get to choose what your family will be like and what your family circumstances will look like by the daily decisions you make. One of the most important decisions you will ever make is who you choose to be your mate.*

The African family has always been so much more than the European concept of the nuclear family. It is so much more than the father, mother and child(ren). In *Let the Circle Be Unbroken*, Dr. Marimba Ani tells us that the African community and family "includes the dead, the living, and the yet unborn" (Ani, 1980, p. 7). Children are also an integral part of the community. In *Welcoming Spirit Home*, Sobonfu Some tells us that in the community she comes from in Burkina Faso, West Africa, "…we know we cannot have community without children, we cannot have children

Honoring Our Ancestral Obligations

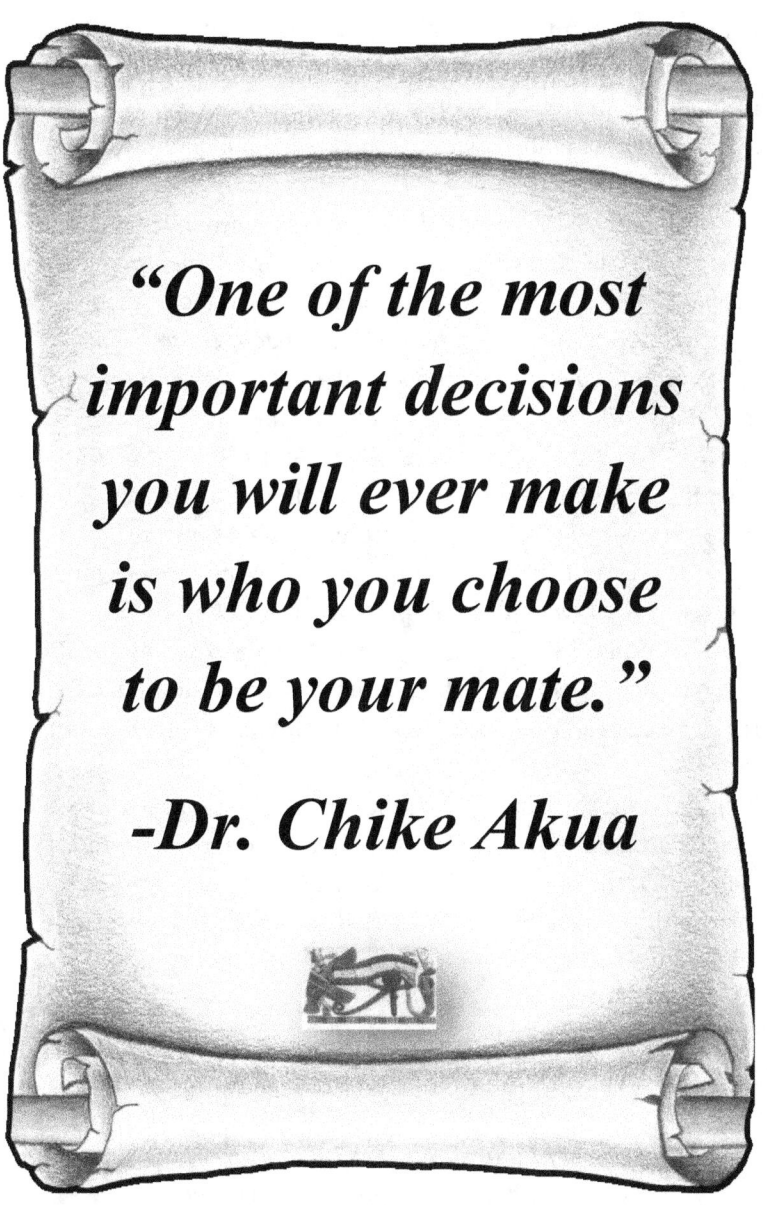

"One of the most important decisions you will ever make is who you choose to be your mate."

-Dr. Chike Akua

without community, and neither would exist without spirit" (Some, 1999, p. 86). Moreover, "the goal of community is to form a diverse body of people with common goals and empower them to embrace their own gifts, selves, and nature" (Some, 1999, p. 29).

Your vision for building a strong family must extend far beyond the trite and trivial relations that far too many young people engage in. This, unfortunately, is what they see many adults engaged in and *much of today's media is aimed at reproducing ungodly relationships based on hyper-materialism and crass, ignorant, sensationalistic behavior.*

You must be very careful how and with whom you spend your time and substance. You will attract what you are, so if, in your life, you want to see more, you must *be* more.

The African family suffered a crippling blow in the midst of the *Maafa*. **The *Maafa* is the catastrophic interruption of African civilization, the great suffering of African people through the American terrorism of captivity (enslavement), lynching, castration, rape, segregation and family separation** (Ani, 1980). This experience for the past four hundred plus years has altered the course of how Black families are constructed. The best White minds of America and Europe were put to the task of destroying African people, families, relationships and culture. "Any system that deprives a people of its family structure, denies the humanity of that people" (Williams 2010, p.7)

Consider the words of Henry Berry from the Virginia House of Delegates in 1832:

> *...we have as far as possible closed every avenue by which light may enter their minds.* We only have to go one step further to extinguish their capacity to see the light and our work will be completed. And they would

then be reduced to the level of the beasts of the field...
(Browder, 1996, p. 116).

Know that whenever you see an intact Black family, a loving Black male/female relationship or marriage—know that you are literally looking at a miracle. Make no mistake about it—Black Love is Black Power!

Cultivating Healthy Relationships

Great families begin with great relationships between the parents. Great relationships are based on shared visions and shared values. They are determined by similar goals of where each person is striving to go (vision) and the guiding beliefs and practices they will use to get there (values). Also, great relationships are built on friendship, mutual respect and honesty.

Many people don't know what a healthy, respectful, functional relationship looks like because they've never seen one. They may have only seen dysfunctional or abusive relationships growing up and therefore do not know how to cultivate a loving relationship. Regrettably, popular media and social media re-circulates some of the same toxic and traumatic images as so-called "entertainment." Building loving relationships is not easy. It requires us to cultivate new skills such as thoughtfulness, empathy, focus, increased discipline, anger management, conflict resolution and much more. Relationships can be complex. But here are a few simple relationship suggestions to live by.

Seven Relationship Suggestions

1. **Take the time to get to know a person.** The most successful relationships tend to be the ones where the couple are friends first or they cultivate a friendship in their romantic relationship. But often, people engage in sexual activity before they get to truly know one another. They may find that they are incompatible because they did not take the time to get to know one another first.
2. **Be honest and faithful.** Great relationships are built on trust and trust is cultivated through honesty. Be honest with the person you are interested in. And if you are in a relationship, be faithful. Dishonesty and infidelity in a relationship can cause immeasurable emotional scars that last a lifetime. Treat your mate as you would like to be treated.
3. **Examine the values a person lives by.** Be clear about your values and take the time to learn the guiding principles a person lives by. Faith in God, hard work and education are a few time-tested values that African Americans have used to find success. Unity, self-determination, respect for Elders are other important values. What values do you cherish most and what values do you desire your mate to have?
4. **Keep your standards high.** Do not settle for someone just because they may be attractive or available. Make sure that they are a person of good character who is striving for excellence, just as you should be striving for the same.
5. **Be mindful of what you're attracted to.** Are you attracted to people who bring out the worst in you? Are you attracted

to people who are engaged in self-destructive habits? Are you attracted to people who are verbally, emotionally or physically abusive? Are you attracted to successful people? Are you attracted to a person of faith?

6. **Seek a person you can build with.** Great relationships are often the result of two people who are building something together: a family, a home, a business, a lifestyle, etc. While physical attraction is important, it is not enough to make a relationship last. Lasting relationships are based on compatibility that comes from a shared commitment to work together.
7. Do not play with a person's emotions. Do not act as if you are interested or attracted to someone if you are not. Do not string a person along as a joke or just because you like the attention. Similarly, if someone is attracted to you and you are not attracted to them, be thoughtful and respectful even if you are not interested in them.

Sometimes it can be very lonely when you haven't found the right person to be in a relationship with. Sometimes a person settles for less simply because they deeply desire a mate and do not want to be alone. But there is an African proverb which says, "It is better to travel alone than with a bad companion." If you have not found a suitable companion, then use your time to develop yourself spiritually, intellectually, emotionally and physically so that when the right person comes along, you will be ready for a functional and fruitful relationship.

There is an African concept called Ubuntu which is embodied in the African Proverb which says, "I am because we are. Because we are, therefore, I am" (Mbiti, 1992). This proverb embodies the connectedness of the community that made us great as a people. There is also an often quoted, but little understood African Proverb which says, *"It takes more* than a mother and father to raise a child. It takes a village to raise a child." If you are going to raise positive, productive children, you had better be clear about who's in your community and who you want to be a part of your village.

Ancient Africans have always had a deep respect for sexual union and life. Their respect for these things was represented in their languages and symbols.

Perhaps humanity's oldest representation of this respect can be found in the ancient African symbol, the ankh. It comes from the Nile Valley nation of Kemet (Egypt) in Africa. The ankh is a symbol of everlasting life. But it also represents the profound respect ancient Africans had for the male and female reproductive organs, and the tremendous power humans have to create new life. The loop at the top of the ankh represents the womb of a woman. This is the place in the woman's body where the baby is nourished and nurtured to life. The two bars extending from beneath the loop represent the ovaries. The ovaries are the female sexual organs which produce eggs.

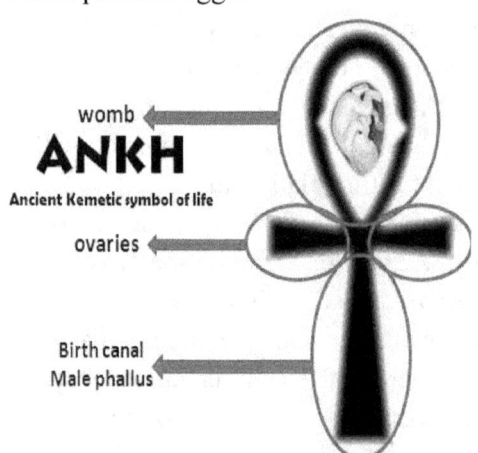

The shaft extending from the ovaries in the ankh represents the birth canal, the path the newborn baby travels as (s)he is being born into this world. It also represents the male phallus or penis.

XIIIIXIIIIXIIIIXIII   Chike Akua, Ph.D.   **XIIIIXIIIIXIIIIXIII**

This symbol was not seen as something funny, odd or obscene. It was seen as a symbol which represented the deep respect African people had for the process of procreation

So it was clear to ancient Africans that sexual responsibility could bring forth life. Sexual irresponsibility could bring forth death. We must return to the traditional ways of our Ancestors. This allowed us to have loving families and communities that stayed together, prospered greatly and were free from crime and violence.

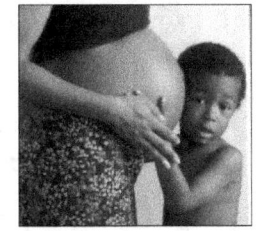

When adults want to convince youth not to have sex, they usually start by telling you lots of horror stories about the negative effects of engaging in premarital sex. But I'm going to begin by teaching a few things that most don't tell youth.

Sex is:
1. Natural: it's how we got here
2. Personal: Because it's personal, it's not advisable to share your relationship business with too many people. Only those trustworthy and wise should be confided in.
3. Beautiful: Sex is a special form of intimacy that should be reserved for someone that is special to you *and* one who regards you as special.
4. Enjoyable: It feels good! There's nothing quite like it when it's with the right person!
5. Wonderful: It feels great! When it's with the right person and at the right time in your life, few things compare!

6. <u>Incredible</u>: How awesome and miraculous it is to think about the fact that the union of a male and female can create new life.
7. <u>Essential</u>: It's necessary for the continuation of life and healthy functioning (Akua, 2012).

But if you are not *thoughtful, practical,* and *responsible,* sex can be:

1. **HARMFUL**: AIDS is running rampant, especially among African American youth; there are also other STDs (sexually transmitted diseases) that one can contract such as syphilis, genital lice (crabs), herpes, and gonorrhea.
2. **PAINFUL**: When a person engages in sex without being thoughtful, practical, and responsible, it can be emotionally painful if things don't work out. Especially in instances of unwed or unwanted pregnancy, sex can be a life-altering choice.
3. **DETRIMENTAL**: Sex does not necessarily make a relationship better. As a matter of fact, it can often cause problems in a relationship and make the relationship more unstable and thus detrimental (Akua, 2012).

Arguably, sex is best reserved for marriage in which two people have made a responsible, loving *commitment*. To many people, this is old-fashioned and outdated. But many of the challenges we face relative to inappropriate and broken relationships and past emotional pains could be alleviated with greater sexual discipline and responsibility.

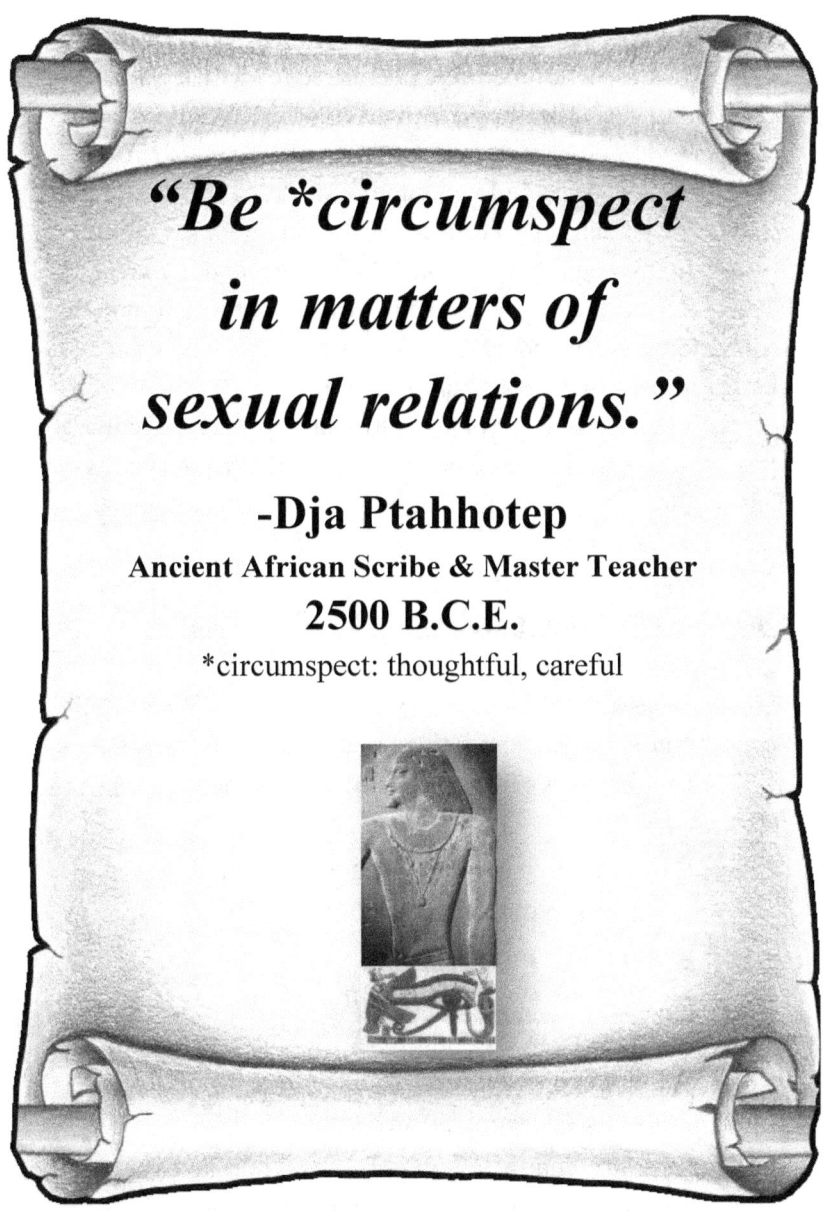

> "Be *circumspect in matters of sexual relations."
>
> -Dja Ptahhotep
> Ancient African Scribe & Master Teacher
> 2500 B.C.E.
>
> *circumspect: thoughtful, careful

People often engage in sexual activity and seek to develop that aspect of their lives before seeking their purpose for being on the planet, getting educated, spiritually-centered, and preparing for a prosperous and productive career. As a result, they oftentimes bring children into the world before they are ready to be parents. This causes a heavy strain on the family.

In my book, *Sexceptional: The Ultimate and Essential Teen Guide to Abstinence*, I give a great deal of insight into these issues along with practical suggestions for those who want to abstain from sexual activity until marriage.

We must build strong, healthy families that are culturally conscious, spiritually-centered and economically prosperous. This requires study, preparation, wisdom, insight and great discipline.

Questions for Thought, Reflection & Discussion

1. What kind of family did you grow up in? What would you like your family to be like ten years from now?
2. In what ways has the Black Family been under siege?
3. Explain why seeing an intact Black male/female relationship or an intact Black family, you are looking at a miracle.
4. Explain the symbolism of the ankh.
5. What were you taught about sex at home?
6. What were you taught about sex at school or in a faith-based organization?
7. Explain what Ptahhotep means when he says, "Be circumspect in matters of sexual relations."

Step 7

Health & Wellness Resuscitation

*We have an Ancestral Obligation
to resuscitate and restore health, wellness and
natural living practices.*

DWENNIMEN
"ram's horns"
"the ram utilizes its heart and not its horns for strength"

*This section is not intended to diagnose or treat illness.
See a qualified medical professional as needed.

When I moved to Atlanta in 1996, I began having serious problems with my sinuses and throat. I was constantly congested, losing my voice and getting sinus infections and respiratory ailments. It was affecting my ability to be effective as a teacher. I went to see the doctor. After describing my symptoms, the doctor checked my vitals. I was then promptly told that I had allergies.

"I've never had problems with allergies before," I responded.

"Well, you do now!" the doctor laughed.

"How could that be?" I asked confused.

"Atlanta is the allergy capital of America. Ear, Nose and Throat doctors come here to specialize," the doctor explained.

"So how do I get rid of the allergies?" I asked.

"You don't get rid of them. You're going to have them until you get to heaven," I was told.

I *could not* and *did not* accept this answer. The doctor then prescribed some antibiotics to clear up the sinus infection and some allergy medication that I was to take indefinitely, unto perpetuity, or "until I got to heaven."

There are many good and well-meaning healthcare professionals who work diligently to try to help people. I salute those who have helped me and countless others, particularly in emergency situations. Their job is not easy. This is not an attempt to discredit sincere people who take their training and their jobs seriously. It is, however, an attempt to call attention to some serious practical and philosophical challenges with western medicine that are not serving us well as a people.

This, along with other health challenges, led me on a quest to find true health, wellness and vitality. Rather than take the allergy medication the doctor prescribed, I started doing research. I discovered that milk and milk-based products produce mucous. Excess mucous causes sinus infections and the other respiratory ailments I was suffering from. I stopped consumption of milk and many milk-based products. I cut back on my intake of cheese and other dairy products. I then supplemented my diet with certain vitamins and minerals; the sinus infections and respiratory ailments disappeared. By educating myself and making incremental changes to my diet, I was able to produce dramatic results in my health. This experience taught me that much of western medicine is aimed at treating symptoms rather than truly solving problems.

Take a mental snapshot of your family—everyone—including mother, father, sisters, brothers, aunts, uncles and grandparents. How are they doing? How is their health? Before the *Maafa*, the catastrophic interruption of African civilization by way of forced removal, captivity, etc, African people lived off the land. We cultivated and consumed fresh fruits and vegetables. The meats we rarely ate were fresh, not injected with hormones and chemicals. In addition, we wrote the world's first medical texts such as the *Ebers Medical Papyrus*, the *Edwin Smith Papyrus* and the *Boulek Papyrus*, all of which documented our deep knowledge of anatomy, physiology, health, healing, and nutrition (Afrika, 1998; Finch, 1998). Fast-forward to today.

Today, as a result of being assimilated and acculturated into American society and partaking in the Standard American Diet (S.A.D.), African Americans suffer disproportionately from high blood pressure, diabetes, obesity and kidney failure which requires dialysis. Indeed, Americans, in general, suffer greatly from these health challenges. However, it is often said that "If

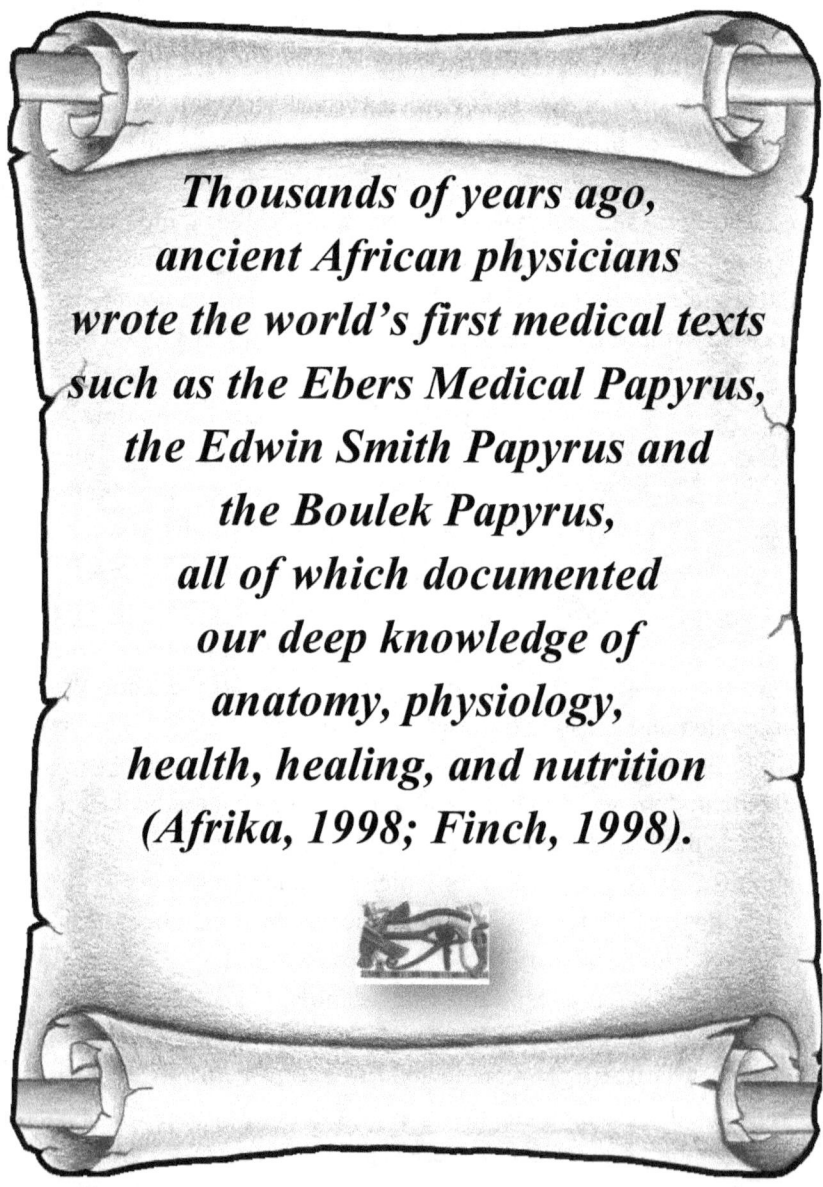

Thousands of years ago, ancient African physicians wrote the world's first medical texts such as the Ebers Medical Papyrus, the Edwin Smith Papyrus and the Boulek Papyrus, all of which documented our deep knowledge of anatomy, physiology, health, healing, and nutrition (Afrika, 1998; Finch, 1998).

America has a cold, we catch the flu." This simply means that whatever ills America has, we experience them in a deeper and more deleterious way than other Americans.

The above medical epidemics notwithstanding, *it is critical to note that if, there seems to be certain medical issues that predominate in your family, this is not a death sentence to you. You can make dietary and lifestyle changes that can help you lead a long and productive life.*

As a result of the many health challenges we face today, many conscious people are beginning to grow their own food, cut back on or remove meat and dairy products from their diet and make their lifestyle more reflective of the way nature intended.

Now, back to that mental picture of your family—are any of the above-mentioned health challenges in your family? African people have always had a completely different way of approaching health and wellness than western medicine. In *Afrikan Holistic Health*, Dr. Llaila Afrika explains:

> Europeans treat the mind in a psychiatric clinic, the spirit in church, and the body in a hospital; while African science includes the body, mind and spirit as a whole—wholistically" (Afrika, 1998, p. 15).

Dr. Afrika goes on to explain additional differences between European medicine and traditional African approaches to wellness:

> European orthodox medicine – use of synthetic drugs and surgery – is organized to treat symptoms. African medicine was organized wholistically to treat the physical, mental, spiritual causes of disease" (Afrika, 1998, p. 15).

The western orientation to health, wellness and disease prevention differs greatly from the African approach. In addition, the Standard American Diet (S.A.D), heavily laden with sugar, salt and fats makes us prime candidates for what Dr. Afrika calls *Nutricide*, "the deliberate and systematic alteration of foods in order to cause physical and mental diseases, genetic mutations and/or death" (Afrika, 2000, p. 19).

These nutritional deficiencies are wreaking havoc on our children, as well. Childhood obesity is a chronic issue which has reached epidemic proportions. Nutritional deficiencies also severely effect behavior. In a society which tells us to "Just Say No" to drugs, we are then coerced to putting our children on highly addictive prescription drugs. **Dr. Jawanza Kunjufu notes, *"about 80 to 85 percent of ADHD children receive drugs while only half of that number receive behavioral and educational modifications."*** He goes on to note that one of the drugs often prescribed is Ritalin and is regarded as "kiddie cocaine." He further observes,

> *"There are signs near schools stressing that drugs cannot be sold or distributed within a one-to-two block radius; yet the biggest drug dealer in the community seems to be our own public school system"* (Kunjufu, 2005, p. 160).

Make no mistake about it—food is a drug when it is produced in a laboratory. Could this be why the agency that regulates what Americans eat is called the Food and Drug Administration? "It must be remembered that foods (synthetic or natural) are chemicals. All chemicals influence the body, mind, mood, and consciousness either positively or negatively" (Afrika, 2000, p. 24). Imagine the irony of overconsumption, yet being nutritionally deprived. *The food-like substances that many consume are saturated with chemicals that have addictive properties. They keep you coming back for more.* Again, these food-like substances are drugs. "Everything chewed is not food...we are nutrient starved people being chased by a chemically-driven society..." (McCauley, 2014, p. 8). Self-care must now take precedence over health care. We must take responsibility for our health.

This begs a very pointed question: Do you eat food or food-like substances? Food can best be described as that which is ingested to sustain life, provide energy and /or promote healthy growth. Food-like substances are unnatural, highly processed substances that slowly degenerate life, energy and health. Food-like substances are available cheap and in great abundance at every turn. But to find and ingest real food on a regular basis, you must be very intentional. For many, it requires a lifestyle change. "Mother Nature is calling us back, because convenience has caused us to stray much too far. She is calling us back to that which was from the beginning" (McCauley, 2014, p. 10).

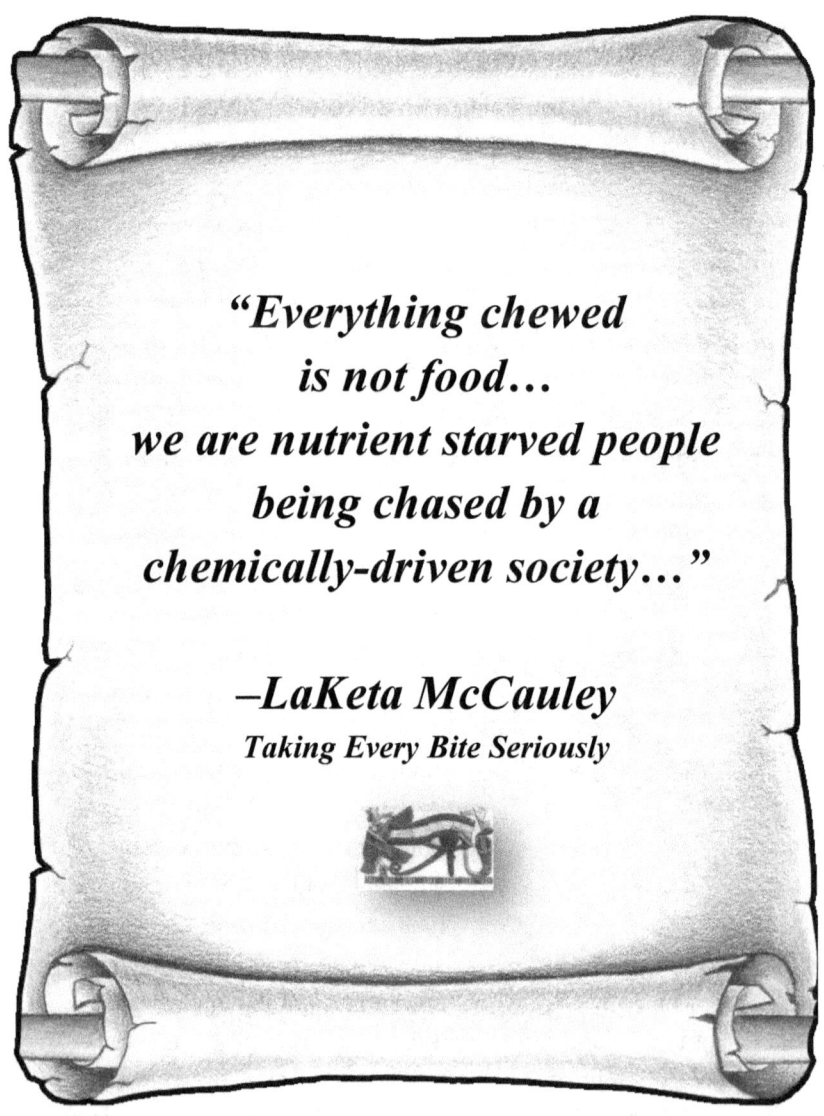

> "Everything chewed is not food... we are nutrient starved people being chased by a chemically-driven society..."
>
> –LaKeta McCauley
> *Taking Every Bite Seriously*

It is critical that we receive our daily intake of fruits and vegetables. Too many people may not be likely to choose fruits and vegetables over high sugar and sodium snacks. *One of the reasons is because these foods are chemically addictive. Changing eating habits is not easy. However, small, incremental changes and additions to the diet can have dramatic long-term positive effects.* This is not optional, but *essential.*

I am not a medical doctor and cannot legally diagnose health problems or cures. Especially in light of the COVID-19 pandemic (and additional pandemics that are projected) it is critical that we be very intentional about maximizing our health habits. For increased health, wellness, energy, and vitality, research shows that there are some simple dietary steps you can take to increase health and longevity:

1. **Drink more water.** This is critical. The body is a chemical factory whose processes are mediated by water. Our bodies are 70-90% water. Many people are walking around dehydrated every day and don't even know it. If a person feels "thirsty" they have been dehydrated much longer than they realize. Sodas, juices, sports drinks and flavored water are not substituteS for *pure* water.

2. **Be sure to get daily fruits and vegetables (especially leafy green vegetables like kale, spinach or romaine lettuce).** Isn't it interesting that snacks and drinks are often fruit-flavored (strawberry, orange, grape, lemon), but we rarely actually eat the fruits that contain the real natural flavor? One way to ensure consistent intake of fruits is blending a fruit smoothie for breakfast every morning.

3. **Take a multivitamin and supplement your diet with essential vitamins and nutrients.** The foods we eat tend not to have the essential vitamins and minerals we need. Even if your family were only eating fruits and vegetables, the soil out of which these natural foods grow has been depleted of essential nutrients.

4. **Be mindful of how often you eliminate.** You should have a bowel movement after every meal, just like a baby does. If your elimination schedule is not this regular, that means toxins (poisons) are being stored in your body creating a climate for fat to increase and disease to flourish.

> "Excess weight (fat) is actually extra cells the body has to maintain. These cells are homes for toxic waste. It is also a waste of bodily energies…Fat becomes a storage place for waste and inhibits the cell's abilities to regain health" (Afrika, 1998, p. 35).

5. **Be active. Engage in a regular exercise routine.** Exercise is essential to optimal functioning and peak potential. Be

mindful that much of the modern western lifestyle has people sitting behind a desk looking at computer screens. Some people even think that sitting in front of a TV playing video games all day is recreation. This can be accomplished by simply walking 20 minutes a day as a low-impact workout. Aerobics, biking and swimming are also great options. Practicing yoga or tai chi is also a wonderful way to promote health, vitality and longevity. These kinds of activities are not optional, but essential.

Mastering Our Mental Health

*This section is not intended to diagnose or treat mental illness or take the place of counseling or therapy. See a qualified counselor or therapist as needed.

In past generations, a stigma was attached to mental illness that made it unacceptable to talk about in public, unless it was the butt of jokes. Many suffered in silence and still many suffer in silence. But now, it is becoming more common and acceptable to seek counseling and therapy and to talk candidly about our issues.

In recent years, a number of high-profile Black athletes have disclosed that they struggled with depression and/or needed counseling and therapy. Some of those athletes include tennis players Serena Williams and Naomi Osaka, Olympic gymnast, Simone Biles, NBA players Paul George, DeMar DeRozan, Marcus and Markieff Morris, to name a few. Money and stardom is not a cure for mental health issues and concerns.

In the book *Unpacking the Emotional Suitcase*, Tierica Berry describes the emotional suitcase as "a metaphor to describe the place where you store painful,

"Trauma not transformed is trauma transferred."

-Tabitha Mpamira-Kaguri

embarrassing or emotionally traumatic experiences" (Berry, 2016, p. 20). Many people are walking around with an emotional suitcase that begins to weigh them down as if they were carrying a bag full of bricks. As a result, they may appear angry, sad, bitter or grumpy and not even know why. In addition, many people's emotional processing system is clogged as they avoid or don't know how to process past or recurring trauma. Some even transfer and circulate trauma and dysfunction to others because their own trauma has been unaddressed. As Tabitha Mpamira-Kaguri says, ***"trauma not transformed is trauma transferred."*** Getting to the source of trauma can be a painful process, but it can also be liberating and transformative.

    Have you ever seen a family member, friend or loved one experience depression or anxiety? Have *you* yourself ever experienced depression or anxiety? Take a mental snapshot of your family. Were there or are there patterns of mental illness or instability? Would you know the signs if you saw them? Some *abnormal* behaviors may seem normal because we saw these behaviors so frequently.

    Also, because certain behaviors were normalized, we may not realize (from a mental health standpoint) what we were really witnessing. But explosive, uncontrollable anger, physical, sexual or emotional violence and abuse, drug and alcohol abuse, sexually risky behavior, heavy emotional mood swings, deep prolonged sadness and violent crimes are just a few examples of abnormal behavior. However, as a people, we have normal and natural problems that have been deeply aggravated by racism (Karenga, 2002).

    We are dealing with intergenerational, multi-generational, unaddressed trauma. And we have struggled for

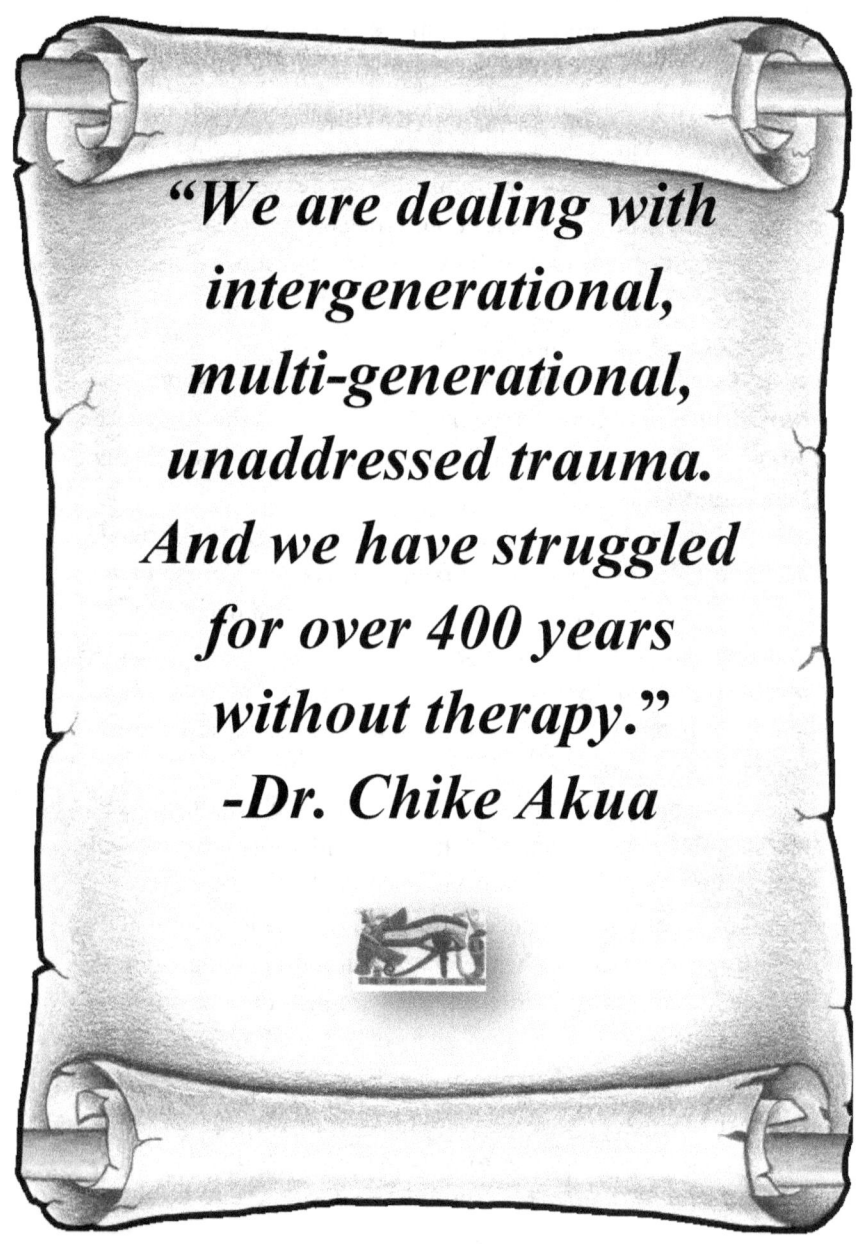

"We are dealing with intergenerational, multi-generational, unaddressed trauma. And we have struggled for over 400 years without therapy."
-Dr. Chike Akua

over 400 years without therapy. Trauma as defined by the DSM-5 (the *Diagnostic and Statistical Manual-5* that psychologists, counselors and psychiatrists use to diagnose patients) defines trauma as, "actual or threatened death, serious injury, or sexual violence." The constant physical, sexual, emotional abuse and daily terrorism of oppression was largely unaddressed generation to generation for over 400 years.

There are many toxic behaviors occurring in our community which are mistaken for our culture. Resmaa Menakem, author of *My Grandmother's Hands: Racialized Trauma and the Pathway to Mending Our Hearts and Bodies* informs us that, **trauma in a people, over time, can look like culture** (Menakem, 2017). And unfortunately, as Baba T'Shango Mbilishaka says, **"African people, without their culture, relate to one another through their trauma."** So we must be very intentional about minding our mental health.

Reuters reported that, overall, severe depression and anxiety rates doubled over the last decade prior to the COVID-19 pandemic from 2007-2018 (https://www.reuters.com/article/us-health-mental-undergrads/depression-anxiety-rising-among-u-s-college-students-idUSKCN1VJ25Z). "In the fall of 2020, 47% of college students reported depression and/or anxiety, according to a University of Michigan Healthy Minds Study. And a recent survey of freshmen at the University of North Carolina at Chapel Hill found a 48% increase in the rates of moderate to severe depression since the pandemic began" (https://store.optum.com/blog/article/mental-health/depression-college-students-why-it-happens-pandemics-role-and-how-help/).

The above statistics are not based on race. But when we focus on the African American community, it is said that if America has a cold, we catch the flu. This simply means that

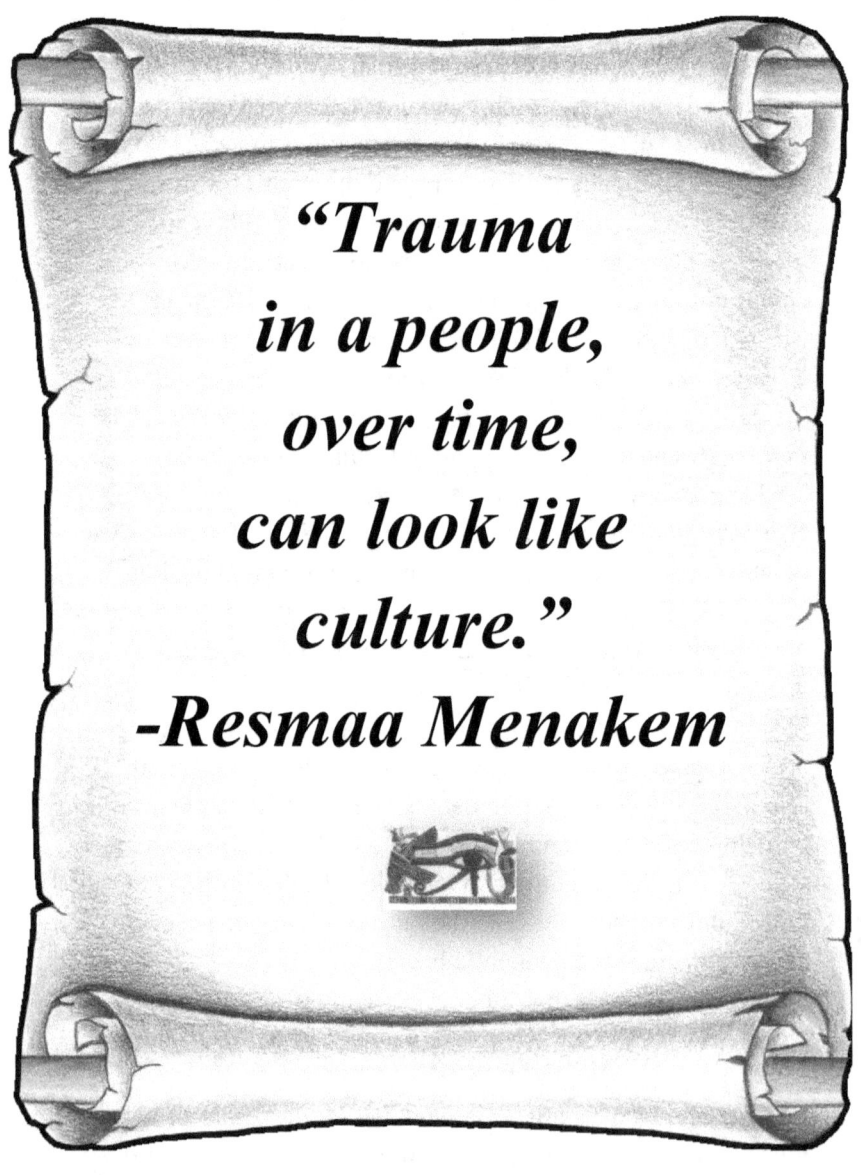

what affects America tends to affect African Americans much more severely. For example, over 18% of persons in the U.S. who experience mental health challenges are African American, but African Americans account for only 12% of the population (Washington, 2019).

It is no secret that though America is considered one of the most advanced nations in the world, it also has one of the highest rates of depression and mental illness in the world. It is also no secret that African Americans experience higher rates of depression, anxiety and mental illness than Whites and others. This has been shown to be due in large part to the increased stresses that racism produces, including poverty, unemployment or underemployment, food insecurity, housing insecurity, violence, police brutality and other factors. Dr. Kevin Washington refers to these factors as Persistent Enslavement Systemic Trauma (PEST) and it occurs when African Americans are surrounded by constant reminders of the danger of being Black (Washington, 2019). This transgenerational trauma often goes untreated. Research shows that African Americans are *least likely* to pursue mental health counseling and therapy, though we suffer most and need it most. This is often stated without explaining the reason *why*.

African Americans have had a toxic relationship with the mental health community from its inception. Early on, in the genesis of the discipline of psychology, and even today, African Americans are often mis-diagnosed and mis-medicated. In addition, early on, sane and natural responses to oppression were deemed to be insanity. For example, in 1851, Samuel Cartwright presented a paper to the Medical Association of Louisiana entitled, "Diseases and Peculiarities of the Negro Race." In it, he coined the term *draptomania* and defined it as a mental illness that caused enslaved Africans to run away. To be clear,

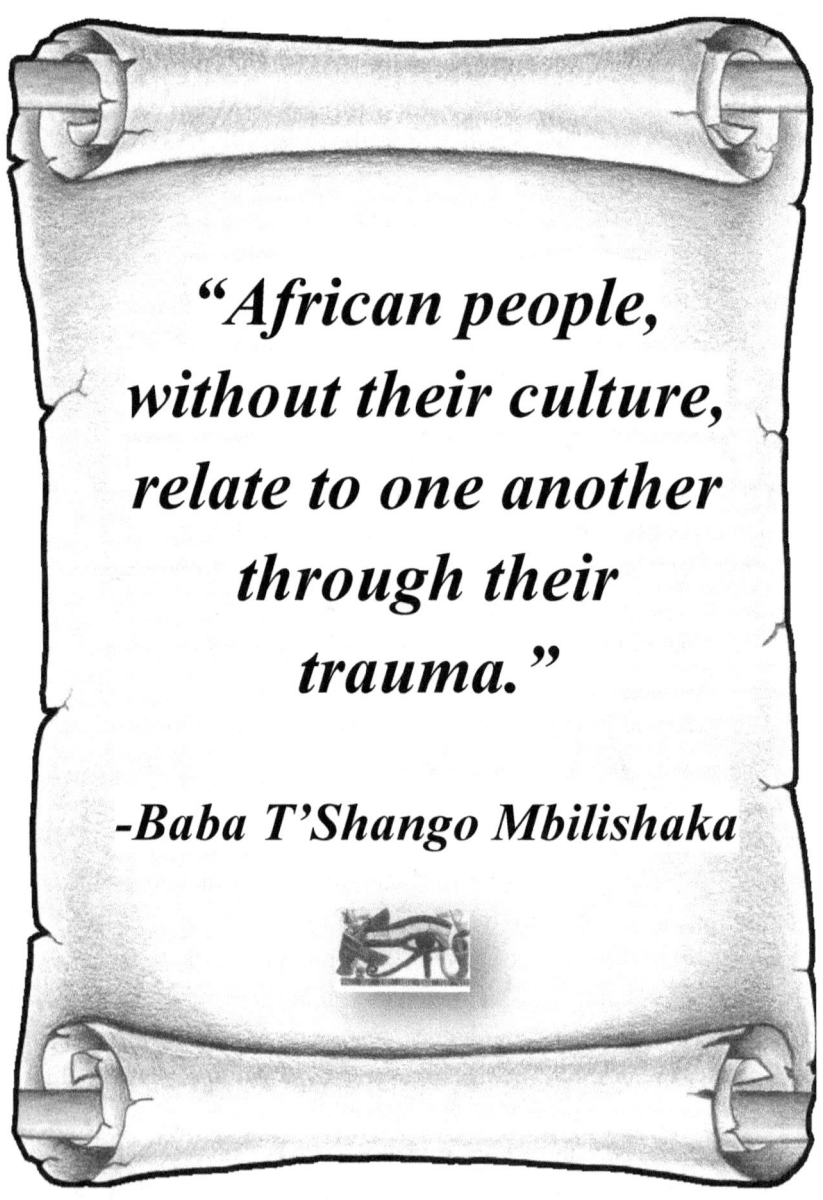

> "African people, without their culture, relate to one another through their trauma."
>
> —Baba T'Shango Mbilishaka

revolting, resisting or running away from oppression and abuse is a natural and sane response to oppression. But Cartwright and others diagnosed a *sane* response to oppression as *insanity*.

When Malcolm X was a child, his father was an outspoken preacher and follower of Marcus Garvey. He preached about Black self-reliance and determination. Their house was set on fire and his father was ultimately murdered by the Klan. In his autobiography, Malcolm X indicated that he felt certain that the murder of his father and the separation of his family by state social workers led to his mother's mental breakdown and subsequent detainment in a mental hospital.

The above are just a few examples of why there is deep distrust of the mental health workers in the Black community. The psychological abuses against Black people and people of color have been so egregious that in October, 2021, the American Psychological Association (APA) issued an apology to people of color for promoting, perpetuating and failing to challenge racism and racial discrimination (https://www.apa.org/about/policy/racism-apology). The APAs racism was the reason why some Black Psychologists left the organization or never joined it and started the Association of Black Psychologists in 1968 to address the needs of Black psychologists and the larger community.

Just as there is a critical shortage of Black teachers, there is also a critical shortage of Black counselors and therapists. Often, when Blacks do receive counseling and therapy, it is with a non-Black counselor or therapist who understands little about our culture and experiences. These are just a few examples of why Blacks have had an unhealthy relationship with the mental health community.

However, *we should not use any of the above information as an excuse to not seek counseling and therapy when it is needed.* We must ask and seek the help we need and don't stop until we find it. So *if you feel like you could benefit from counseling, you are not alone.* To find qualified therapists, check out www.BlackTherapistsRock.com. Psychology is the science of human behavior that serves as a foundation for counseling and therapy. Interestingly, the word psychology comes from the Greek term *psyche* meaning "soul." Further, the Greek word psyche comes from the ancient Kemetic (Egyptian) word *sakhu* which means, "illumination of the spirit" (Nobles, 2006, p. *xxvi*). So an effective psychology is a science of the soul and the illumination of the spirit. This can and should be part of the ultimate goal of counseling and therapy, though the immediate goal may be to help a person simply function more effectively without anxiety or uncontrollable anger or any number of other mental disorders.

In ancient Kemet, education and the pursuit of wisdom began with *rekh shenu*, "Knowledge of Self." What do you really know about yourself, your body, your health, your emotions, your spirit, your soul, the world and the universe? Education in our original societies and civilizations addressed this and much more. It was understood that increased knowledge and support would help a person make better decisions.

Self-Education v. Self-Medication

Because of an inability to deal with life and past trauma, many people try to self-medicate with drugs and/or alcohol. But we should *self-educate* instead of self-medicate. Did you know that *all the chemicals you need to feel high are already in your*

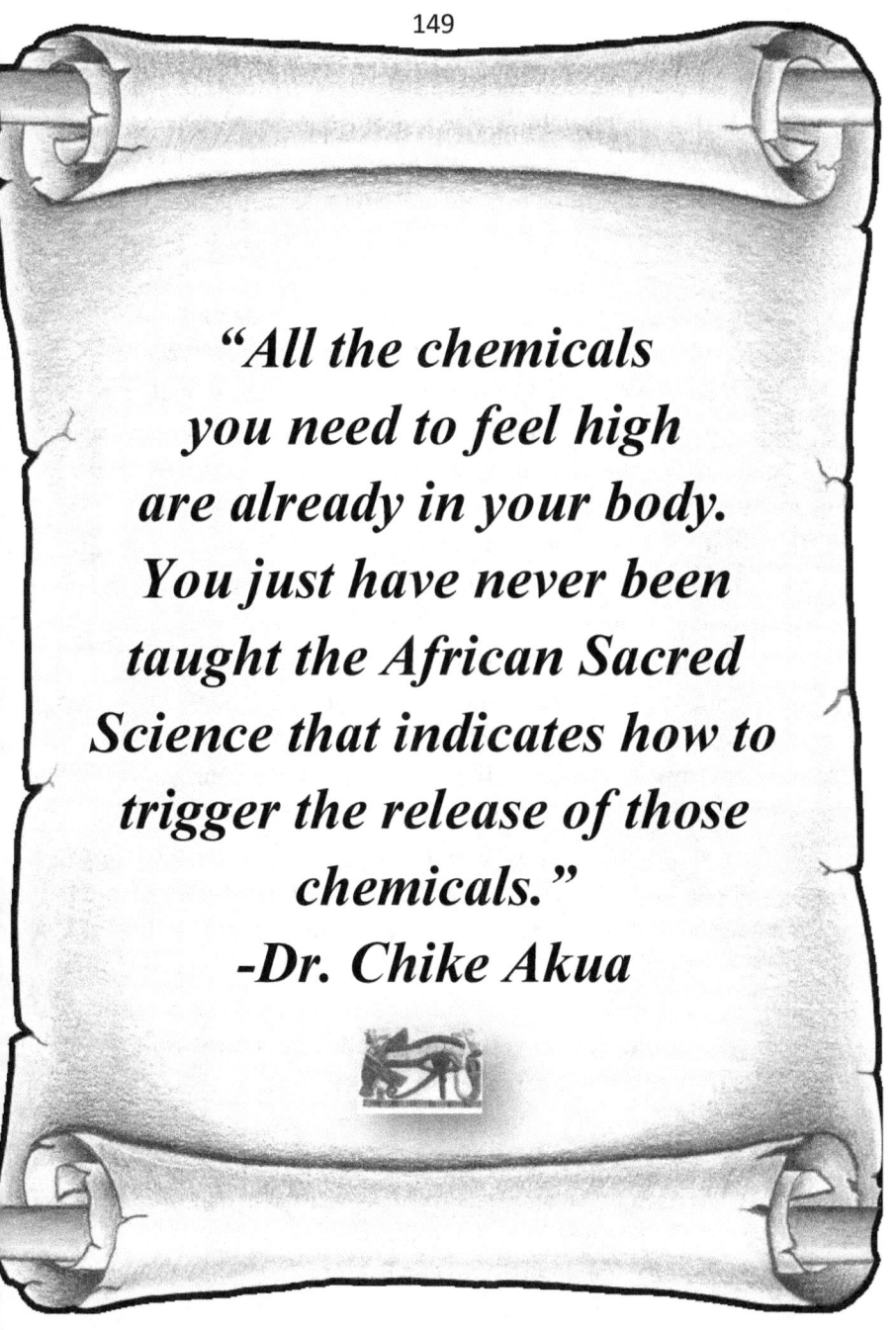

"All the chemicals you need to feel high are already in your body. You just have never been taught the African Sacred Science that indicates how to trigger the release of those chemicals."
-Dr. Chike Akua

body? You just have never been taught the African Sacred Science that indicates how to trigger the release of those chemicals! Most people are just completely unaware and look for artificial, harmful substitutes. Again, the feel-good chemicals that produce feelings of love, joy, oneness, peace and pleasure are already in your body.

Whether smoking marijuana, drinking alcohol excessively or even over-eating, it is often used as a form of avoidance to escape and/or numb unaddressed emotional pain. It's self-medication. *We must engage in self-education instead of self-medication.* Though marijuana was used ceremonially and medicinally among African and indigenous people and though it has been legalized in many states, it is often laced with very harmful and addictive chemicals unbeknownst to the person consuming it—until it's too late.

First, we must ***mind*** our mental health. This means becoming more aware and more educated about the issues within ourselves, our families and communities. Second, we must ***mend*** our mental health. This means having the courage to engage in the process of healing through counseling and/or therapy and removing the stigma attached to it. Once we begin to mind and mend our mental health, then we must ***master*** our mental health. This means making a commitment to healing and overcoming the challenges that past trauma may have created for you and/or your family. It means you ultimately take control over your emotions and your emotions do not control you. Some of the most amazing people on the planet are those that suffered unbelievably severe trauma, but then turned their pain into *power*. And you can, too.

Self-education reveals that the chemicals that produce feel-good feelings are *dopamine, serotonin, anandamide, endorphins, norepinephrine, oxytocin* and *melatonin*. These chemicals are pleasurable, pain blockers, that produce calming and centering feelings and feelings of oneness. We do not need to smoke, drink alcohol or over-eat to feel high or buzzed.

Self-education makes you aware of your own **trauma triggers**, those occurrences that take you in your mind and feelings back to a traumatic experience. Trauma triggers make you feel anxious, angry, fearful, sad, depressed and hopeless. But self-education also indicates that, just as there are trauma triggers, there are also **transformation triggers**. Transformation triggers are thoughts, words and actions that link you to your personal power, faith, courage, self-determination, encouragement, strong values, etc. that help you achieve your desired goals. We can consciously create transformation triggers for ourselves to lift us to higher levels of hope and productivity. Through the foods we eat, the time we spend outside in nature, proper breathing, daily exercise, living righteously and interaction with people on a similar path, we can stimulate the healthy release and flow of transformational chemicals. Be thoughtful and intentional about minding and mending your mental health. On the road to mastering our mental health, we must be intentional about controlling our thoughts, feelings and emotions and not allowing our thoughts feelings and emotions to control us.

9 Simple Suggestions to Improve Your Mental Health

1. Gratitude is the gateway to fulfillment. Begin and end each day by thinking about what you are thankful for. Also, keep an attitude of gratitude throughout your day.
2. Do your best to avoid people and places that are not in alignment with your values and emotions.

3. Daily exercise is known to have a very positive impact on one's mental health. Even just walking a mile or two per day can be deeply beneficial.
4. Take quiet time each day in the morning and evening to do some deep breathing and visualize your goals and dreams. Unplug from all external stimuli (cell phone, TV, social media, etc.). Start with five minutes and increase it to 15 minutes.
5. Share your emotions with someone you trust (a friend or family member). While this cannot and should not be considered a substitute for counseling and therapy, it can be therapeutic. *Don't keep your emotions bottled up.* There are many Elders in our community who have a great deal of wisdom to share and they may have experienced challenging circumstances similar to yours. Do you have someone you trust to share your thoughts and feelings with?
6. Spend time outdoors at least once a day. Lack of sunlight and fresh air is detrimental to your mental health. Conversely, sunshine and fresh air can stimulate the chemicals responsible for feelings of joy, fulfillment and mental health.
7. Studies show that many people experience increased anxiety due to too much screen time. Turn your phone off an hour before going to bed and wait at least 30 minutes before looking at your phone in the morning until after your deep breathing and visualization mentioned above in suggestion #3.
8. Take a mental snapshot of your family, friends and associates and examine patterns of mental health and mental illness. Whose life serves as a healthy model for you?
9. Our culture is the key and our culture is the cure. We are a communal, cooperative and collective people. This is one of the reasons why there is an African Proverb that says, *"A person is a person because there are people."* So being in

community with like-minded brothers and sisters who are seeking to advance themselves in healthy ways is good for your mental health. Such a community could be a faith-based community, a club, a team, an organization, fraternity or sorority. Conversely, spending inordinate amounts of time in racially and mentally toxic environments is hazardous to our mental health and should be avoided at all costs.

*This section was not intended to diagnose or treat a mental illness or take the place of counseling or therapy. See a qualified counselor or therapist as needed.

Mastering Our Melanin

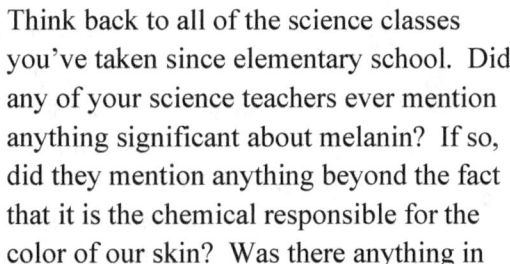

Think back to all of the science classes you've taken since elementary school. Did any of your science teachers ever mention anything significant about melanin? If so, did they mention anything beyond the fact that it is the chemical responsible for the color of our skin? Was there anything in your science book? Your biology book? Your chemistry book? **If not, *why not*?!**

BEFORE AND AFTER

In his book, *Melanin: What Makes Black People Black*, Dr. Laila Afrika suggests that ignorance of our melanin and its functions allows us to be controlled and manipulated as a people. Dr. Afrika refers to melanin as **"the**

chemical key to life." The lack of knowledge surrounding the magnificence of our melanin has caused skin lightening to become a multi-million dollar industry as some Blacks engage in the *self-hating, self-mutilating act of skin bleaching.* While non-Blacks are going to great lengths to sit in tanning spas to darken their skin, skin bleaching among Blacks has become all the rage in many parts of Africa and the Caribbean. Who taught us to hate ourselves in this way. Author Tony Browder has noted that **"There was a time when Blackness was a badge of honor."** Unfortunately, due to ignorance and skillful mis-education, many wear it as an emblem of shame. We must learn to love the skin we're in.

Thankfully, some actors and actresses have emerged who are comfortable with the skin they're in. They demonstrate excellence and elegance simultaneously. This sends a powerful message, especially to young boys and girls that **Black is a beautiful blessing from the Creator.**

In his book, *Dark Matters, Dark Secrets*, Dr. T. Owens Moore has compared melanin in the body to the dark matter of outer space. As much as 90 percent of outer space is dark matter. Dark matter is the space between the stars and other celestial objects. *"Just like dark matter is used in astronomical terms to describe the external universe, melanin is the dark matter of the internal universe (the human body)"* (Moore, 2002, p. 3).

It is no secret that African people have a way of walking, talking, moving, singing, dancing and *being* that evokes a certain sense of mystery among non-Black people. The ways of African people are often imitated but never quite duplicated. African

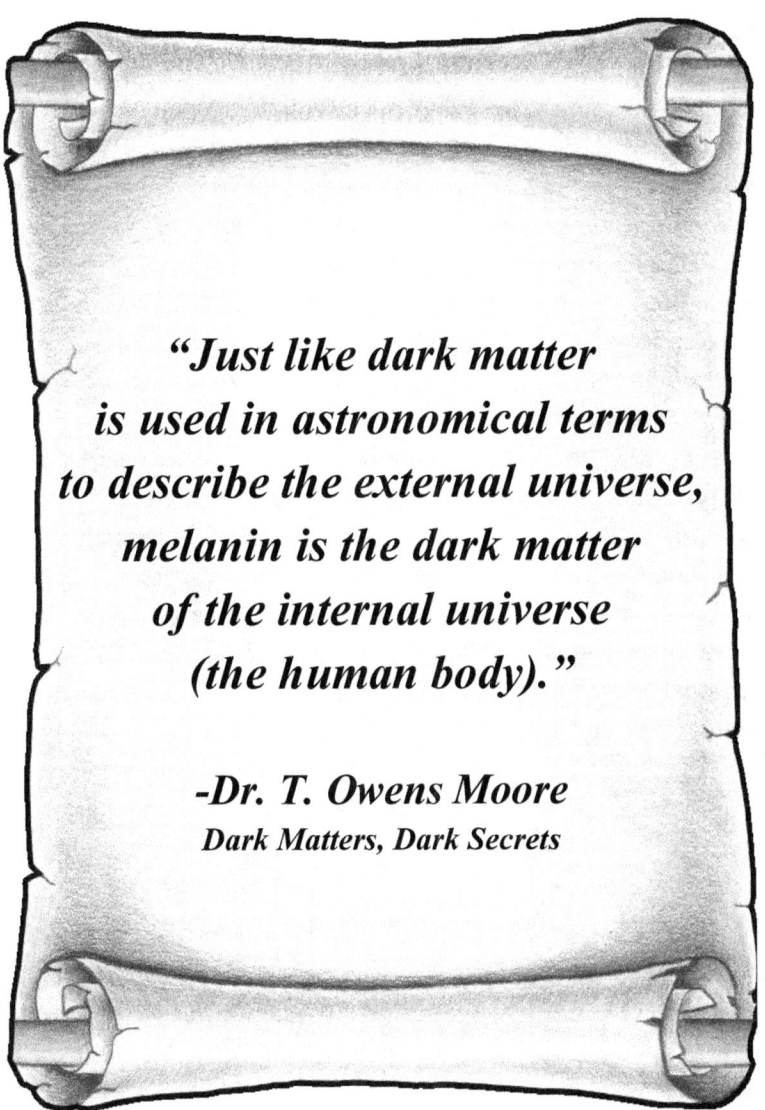

> *"Just like dark matter is used in astronomical terms to describe the external universe, melanin is the dark matter of the internal universe (the human body)."*
>
> -Dr. T. Owens Moore
> *Dark Matters, Dark Secrets*

people and other indigenous people have unique ways of being in the world that have always seemed strange to the western world. Melanin can help to provide insight into some of these mysteries. *All people have melanin, but African people and people of color have higher concentrations of melanin, not just in the skin, but in the brain and other organs of the body.* Higher concentrations of melanin deeply and directly affects physiological functions. We come in many different shapes, sizes and shades. It should be noted that the *concentrations of melanin in the skin, do not always indicate the levels of melanin in the body.*

In addition, improper nutrition can calcify or harden the pineal gland which compromises its power to secrete the hormone melatonin. **Melatonin** is responsible for regulating your body's rhythms and sleep. Many melanin scholars have also done studies which concluded that the pineal gland and its secretion of melatonin are responsible for higher levels of spiritual consciousness and inner vision (Afrika, 1998; King, 1994; Pookrum, 1994).

A serious study of melanin reveals that what we view and listen to has a powerful impact on the melanin in our bodies. Think back to our discussion of the effects of media consumption in previous chapters. Melanin records and stores information. In *Vitamins and Minerals from A to Z,* medical doctor and medical researcher, Dr. Jewel Pookrum explains, *"Melanin is essentially involved in controlling all mental and physical body activities"* (Pookrum, 1999, p. 26).

XIIIIXIIIIXIIIIXIII   Chike Akua, Ph.D.   **XIIIIXIIIIXIIIIXIII**

Melanin comes from the Greek word *melanos,* which means "black" (King, 2001, p. 48). *It is a semiconductor which allows for information to be processed in the brain quickly and efficiently. It is also known to regulate biorhythms.* "It is also in almost every major organ of the body" (Pookrum, 1999, p. 20). Pookrum indicates that "Melanin plays a dominant role in information processing that is essential for proper neurologic and metabolic function" (Pookrum, 1999, p. 28). Medical research has demonstrated that while melanin in the skin is significant, melanin is also a chemical that is found in the iris of the eye, the inner ear, and that there are twelve melanated centers in the brain (King, 2001).

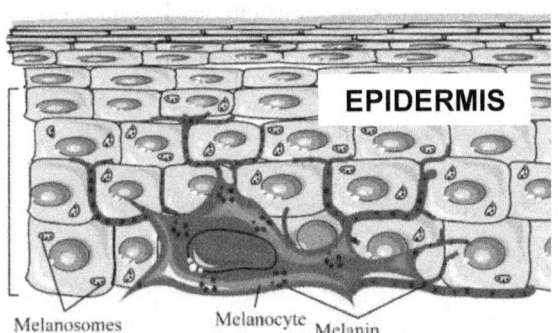

Pookrum also explains that "Melanin is synthesized and distributed by specialized cells, known as **melanocytes**, within the organs of the body" (Pookrum, 1999, p. 22). She goes on to explain that melanin is always contained in a small battery cell known as a **melanosome**" which is contained inside the melanocyte (Pookrum, 1999, p. 23).

Melanin absorbs different forms of light (*even sound*) "and uses them as energy sources to recharge itself and the cells in which it is located…" (Pookrum, 1999, p. 28). Light, then, is a form of nutrition. This is critical when one considers that many people do not get enough sunlight. Sunlight actually has therapeutic effects that impact higher level brain functioning and mental health, especially for melanin-dominant individuals.

In *The African Origins of Biological Psychiatry*, Dr. Richard King demonstrates than ancient Africans had a vast knowledge of melanin and the pineal gland's activity in opening and awakening the *udjat* or Third Eye, the spiritual eye which allows us to see beyond the physical and into the mental and spiritual dimensions. This knowledge was encoded in the design of the mask of King Tutankhamun and other artifacts and ancient writings.

It is these and other thoughts that prompted the poet and visionary television producer, Listervelt Middleton to advise in his poem "On the Origin of Things": "Sharpen your eye and tune your ear, so you know what you see and understand what you hear."

To maximize and master our melanin, we must:
1. **Turn off, tune in and turn on**. *Turn off* external media (radio, TV, computer, tablet, etc.). *Tune into* your inner Higher Self (God). *Turn on* your higher powers of visualization, intuition and manifestation.
2. **Get consistent and proper amounts of sun light.** In most people's fast-paced lifestyle, it is easy to go in and out of buildings everyday or stay inside all day and not get any sunlight. Be very intentional about getting more time in the sun. One way to do this is by stretching, doing deep breathing or exercising outdoors everyday.

3. **Eat foods that feed and nourish your pineal gland and that help produce melanin.** Eat fruits and vegetables like bananas, grapes and dark green, leafy vegetable which contain amino acids like phenylalanine and tyrosine. These are the building blocks of melanin.
4. Carefully regulate the visual and auditory media (TV, music, computers) that you expose yourself to because the light emitted through these sources is stored in your melanin (see #1).

Scripture reveals that we are wonderfully made in the image of the Most High. We should understand the magnificence of how we are created so we can maximize our capacity and manifest our greatness to transform ourselves and humanity.

Questions for Thought, Reflection & Discussion

1. Describe how the author transformed some of his medical issues with dietary changes.
2. Are there any medical conditions which seem to run in your family (high blood pressure, diabetes, obesity, etc.)? How can you combat these issues?
3. Explain what nutricide is.
4. Describe and discuss mental health issues and/or concerns that you have witnessed.
5. What is the difference between trauma triggers and transformation triggers? Explain and give examples of each.
6. Which of the suggestions about improving your mental health resonates with you most? Why?
7. Name at least three ways in which melanin powerful?

Honoring Our Ancestral Obligations

160

Afterword

Walking into Our Destiny & Building for Eternity

XIIIIXIIIIXIIIIXIII Chike Akua, Ph.D. **XIIIIXIIIIXIIIIXIII**

There is an ancient African concept known as *serudj ta*, which means, "restoring the world" (Karenga, 1998, p. 23). It means "to repair that which is damaged; to strengthen that which is weakened; to set right that which is wrong." Hatshepsut, the ancient African woman who ruled Kemet over 3500 years ago, stated, "I have raised up that which was in ruins. I have restored that which was destroyed" (Karenga, 1998, p. 63). This is our calling—to "help restore our people to their traditional greatness."

This process is filled with ups and downs, ins and outs, challenges and trials, and, triumphs and victories. But through it all, never underestimate the power of your life experiences, both good and bad. For example, in my schooling, I underwent a period of chronic underachievement. Starting in 6th grade, my grades fell sharply from As and Bs to Cs and Ds. I even received an F in 8th grade language arts.

It continued through high school where I had a 1.9 GPA going into my senior year. I underwent a dramatic transformation in my senior year and raised a 1.9 GPA to a 3.2 with the help of tutoring and encouragement from my sister. Still, I was barely accepted into Hampton University on probation because of a cumulative GPA of 2.006 and poor SAT and ACT scores. I was informed that if I attended a Summer Bridge Pre-College Program and was a able to maintain a 2.0 GPA, they would accept me as a full-time student.

I'll never forget when my parents took me to the airport to go to the pre-college program at Hampton University. My Dad parked the car and my mom walked me to my gate. All of a sudden, in the middle of the airport, she began crying and calling out to God in prayer. She asked that God would protect me at all times and guide me to become successful.

I got on the plane almost in tears myself and began to think about my journey through childhood from being a good student to a poor student and then one who made the honor roll in my senior year. I began to think about all the sacrifices my parents had made for me. I stepped off the plane that day transformed and on a mission to make my parents and my people proud.

That day I learned the power of prayer as a young man. I later graduated in four years from Hampton University and earned a master's degree from Clark Atlanta University with honors! My journey has come full circle. I currently serve on the faculty in the Department of

Educational Leadership at Clark Atlanta University. *Today I share this story and the others to remind you of the power of purpose, prayer and potential.*

All of this is just the beginning of many great things to come. It has inspired me to write books, produce video content, Black History Posters, online curricula and to travel the country and the world showing students, teachers, parents, and everyday people the beauty of African history and culture through my *African Origins* presentations and books. This precious wisdom that can be gained from the study of African culture can help us in modern times. It can help us heal a world that is in such great need.

We have what it takes to be great. But greatness and success must be redefined for our purposes. Greatness and success is not just getting a good job with benefits. It cannot be found in being able to purchase an abundance of material things.

As you can see from reading this book, **Honoring Our Ancestral Obligations** means:
1. Being culturally conscious.
2. Being spiritually centered.
3. Being economically astute.
4. Being committed to the core.
5. Building for Eternity to leave a lasting legacy.
6. Consistently working for the resurrection of African people
7. And working for the redemption of Humanity.

There is an African Proverb which says, *"The ruin of a nation begins in the homes of its people."* If the ruin of a nation begins in the homes of its people, *then the resurrection of a nation must begin in the home*, as well.

So we must build strong relationships. Strong relationships lead to strong families. Strong families lead to strong communities. Strong communities lead to strong cities. Strong cities lead to strong states. Strong states lead to strong nations. Strong nations lead to a transformed world and a better humanity. But it all begins with YOU…and every decision you make along the way.

Your Ancestors paved the way for you to continue their work. The fact that you have read this book is not by chance. Take it as evidence that you have a Higher Calling to work for the resurrection of African people and the redemption of humanity.

As I stated in the beginning, America has tremendous opportunity. But it also has structured inequity. This never stopped our most revered Ancestors. Our job is to take advantage of the opportunities and transform the inequities. We *can* do this and we *must* do this. As Dr. George Fraser says, "We have the timber…let us build."

If you have read this book from beginning to end and carefully considered the content within it, then you are ready to take the Ancestral Obligation Oath.

Ancestral Obligation Oath

I have come here today in the presence of the Most High and Ancestors.
I have studied a small portion of the culture and heritage of African people and the people of the world.
Though I have learned much, there is still much more to know.

I now accept the call to Higher Consciousness. I am an agent of change and transformation.
I am Ma'at Kheru (True of Voice).
I am a student of exceptional insight seeking enlightenment and illumination.
I am committed to the core.

I pledge to devote myself to the study of who I am.
I pledge to help restore peace to the world in all I think, say and do.
I will not dishonor the memory of my Ancestors nor disrespect the struggles of my Elders by engaging in self-destructive behavior.

I will make my Ancestors proud, for their struggles were not in vain.
Through character, consciousness, competence and commitment, I will awaken my people...
And in awakening my people, I will call all the Human Family back to a state of peace and empowerment.

On this day, I do sincerely make this pledge that my life will be full and fulfilled so that on the day of reckoning, history, humanity and heaven will judge me to be a Noble Soul who balanced the Scales of Ma'at.

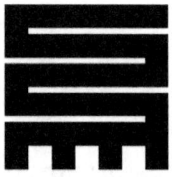

Nkyinkimie
"Selfless Devotion to Service"

Print Name: _____

Signature: _____

Date: _____

References

Afrika, Llaila (1998). *Afrikan holistic health.* NY: A&B Publishers Group.

Afrika, Llaila (2000). *Nutricide: The nutritional destruction of the Black Race.* NY: A&B Publishers Group.

Afrika (2009). *Melanin: What makes Black people black.* Long Island City, NY: Seaburn Publishing Company.

Akbar, Na'im (1991). *Visions for Black men.* Tallahassee, FL: Mind Productions.

Akua, Chike (2012). *Education for transformation: The keys to releasing the genius of African American students.* Imani Enterprises: Conyers, GA.

Akua, Chike (2012). *Sexceptional: The ultimate & essential guide to teen abstinence.* Imani Enterprises: Conyers, GA.

Akua, Chike (2004). *A Kwanzaa awakening: Lessons for the Community* (4th Edition), Imani Enterprises, Conyers, GA.

Ani, Marimba (1980). *Let the circle be unbroken: Implications for African spirituality in the Diaspora.* NY: Nkonimfo Publications.

Asante, Molefi (2007). *An Afrocentric manifesto: Toward an African renaissance.* London: Polity Press.

Asante, Molefi (1988). *Afrocentricty.* Trenton, NJ: Africa World Press.

Baruti, Mwalimu Bomani (2010). *IWA: A warrior's character.* Atlanta, GA: Akoben House.

Berry, Tierica (2017). *Unpacking the emotional suitcase.* Decatur, GA: Affirmative Expression.

Carruthers, Jacob (1995). *Mdw Ntr: Divine speech.* London: Karnak House.

Clarke, John H. (1991). *Notes for an African world revolution: Africans at the crossroads.* Trenton, NJ: Africa World Press.

DeGruy, Joy (2005). *Post traumatic slavery syndrome.* Portland, OR: Joy DeGruy Publications, Inc.

Fenwick, Leslie (2001). *Patterns of excellence: policy perspectives on diversifying teaching and school leadership.* Atlanta, GA: Southern Education Foundation.

Finch, Charles (1998*). The star of deep beginnings: The African genesis of science and technology.* Atlanta, GA: Khenti Press.

Fraser, George (2008). *Click: Ten truths for building extraordinary relationships.* New York: McGraw Hill.

Fuller, Neely, Jr. (1984). *The united independent compensatory code/system/concept: a textbook/workbook for thought, speech and/or action for victims of racism (white supremacy).* Washington, C. C.: Neely Fuller, Jr.

Hilliard, A., Williams, L. & Damali, N. (1987). *The teachings of Ptahhotep: The oldest book in the world.* Atlanta, GA: Blackwood Press.

Hilliard, Asa (1995). *The Maroon Within Us.* Black classic Press, Baltimore, MD.

Hilliard, Asa (2003). *African power: Affirming African indigenous socialization in the face of culture wars.* Tallahassee, FL: Makare Publishing.

Karenga, Maulana (1998): *Kwanzaa: A celebration of family, community, and culture.* Los Angeles, CA: University of Sankore Press.

Karenga, Maulana (1999). *The Odu Ifa: The ethical teachings.* Los Angeles, CA: University of Sankore Press.

Karenga, Maulana (2002). *Introduction to Black studies.* Los Angeles: University of Sankore Press.

Karenga, Maulana (2008). *Kawaida and questions of life and struggle.* Los Angeles: University of Sankore Press.

King, J., Akua, C., Russell, L. (2014). Liberating Urban Education for Human Freedom. In H. Richard Milner & Kofi Lamotey (Eds.), *Handbook of Urban Education* (pp 24-49). New York: Routledge.

King, Joyce, & Swartz, Ellen (2014). *"Re-membering" history in student and teacher learning: An Afrocentric culturally informed praxis.* New York, NY: Routledge.

King, Richard (1994). *The African origins of biological psychiatry.* Newport News, VA: UB & US Communications Systems.

King, Richard (1994). *Melanin: A key to freedom.* Chicago, IL: Lushena Books, Inc.

Kunjufu, Jawanza (1991). *Black economics.* Chicago: African American Images.

Kunjufu, Jawanza (2000). *Satan, I'm taking back my health.* Chicago: African American Images.

Kunjufu, Jawanza (2013). *Keeping Black boys out of special education.* Chicago: African American Images.

McCauley, LaKeta (2014). *Taking every bite seriously*. Novi, MI: Taking Every Bite Seriously, Inc.

Menekem, Resmaa (2017). *My grandmother's hands: Racialized trauma and the pathway to mending our hearts and bodies*. Las Vegas, NV: Central Recovery Press.

Moore, T. Owens (2001). *Dark matters, dark secrets*. Redan, GA: Zamani Press.

Nketsia, Nana Kobina V (2013). *African culture in governance and development: The Ghana paradigm*. Accra, Ghana: Ghana Universities Press.

Nobles, Wade (2006). *Seeking the Sakhu: Foundational writings for an African psychology*. Chicago, IL: Third World Press.

Pookrum, Jewel (1999). *Vitamins and Minerals from A to Z*. Buffalo, NY: Eworld, Inc.

Powell, Alfred (2008). *Hip-Hop hypocrisy: When lies sound like the truth*. New York: NY: iUniverse, Inc.

Robinson, Robinson, & Battle (1989). *Journey of the Songhai people*. Philadelphia, PA: Farmer Press.

Shujaa, Mwalimu (1994). *Too much schooling, too little education: A paradox of Black life in White societies*. Trenton, NJ: Africa World Press.

Some, Sobonfu (1997). *The spirit of intimacy: Ancient teachings in the ways of relationships*. Berkeley, CA: Berkeley Hill Books.

Some, Sobonfu (1999). *Welcoming spirit home: Ancient African teachings to celebrate children and community*. Novato, CA: New World Library.

Williams, Richard (2010). *They Stole It But You Must Return It.* Powder Springs, GA: HEMA Publishing.

Williams, Juan and Ashley, Dwayne (2004). *I'll find a way or make one: a tribute to historically black colleges and universities.* New York: Amistad Press.

Willis, W. Bruce (1995). *The Adinkra Dictionary.* Washington DC: The Pyramid Complex.

Van Sertima, Ivan (2001). *Blacks in science.* Brunswick, NJ: Transaction Publishers.

Woodson, Carter G. (1933). *The Mis-education of the Negro.* Washington D.C.: Associated Publishers.

About Dr. Chike Akua

Chike Akua, Ph.D. is an assistant professor of educational leadership at Clark Atlanta University and one of the most sought after speakers at colleges, universities, educational conferences and urban schools.

Dr. Akua is a leading authority on increasing the achievement of today's students, especially those in the most challenging schools and communities. As a scholar-practitioner, Dr. Akua's research is published in the *Journal of Black Studies* and other scholarly publications. With an African-centered and culturally relevant approach toward closing access and opportunity gaps, he is known for his dynamic, interactive presentations to educational leaders, students and parents.

Dr. Akua earned a Bachelor of Arts degree from Hampton University in Education, a Master of Arts degree in Education with a concentration in school counseling from Clark Atlanta University and a doctorate in Educational Policy Studies from Georgia State University.

Dr. Akua has helped lead over 1000 students and parents on trips throughout Egypt, Ghana, Morocco and Senegal through the **D'Zert Club's Teen Summit 1000** program. Dr. Akua is frequently called upon by education, civic, and social organizations to speak about educational excellence and cultural knowledge.

To book Dr. Chike Akua for a conference keynote speech, workshop or seminar, email DrAkua@DrAkua.net or call (770)309-6664.

XIIIIXIIIIXIIIIXIII   Chike Akua, Ph.D.   **XIIIIXIIIIXIIIIXIII**

Other Books and Posters by Dr. Chike Akua

www.DrAkua.net

Education for Transformation: *The Keys to Releasing the Genius of African American Students*
By Dr. Chike Akua

This book details African-centered and culturally relevant instructional strategies used with some of the most challenging students during Mr. Akua's fourteen years as a public school teacher.
It also documents the most promising practices of Master Teachers he has observed around the country.

Praise for *Education for Transformation:*

Education for Transformation *is a powerfully written book. It was much needed ten years ago when it was first written, but needed even more so now in today's political climate. I consider* Education for Transformation *a must read for any and all leaders and teachers of African American children."*
    Principal Baruti Kafele, Author of
    The Equity & Social Justice Education 50: Critical Questions
    for Improving Opportunities & Outcomes for Black Students

"This book is a must-read for all serious educators who want to get results and understand the connection between culture and achievement."
    Dr. Joyce E. King, Benjamin E. Mays Chair
    Georgia State University

Honoring Our Ancestral Obligations

ParentPower!: The Keys to Your Child's Academic & Social Success
By Dr. Chike Akua

Today, many parents feel like they've lost their power because they are competing for their child's attention amidst many high-tech weapons of mass *distraction*. *ParentPower* gives parents **clear strategies** on how to reclaim their power and how to properly educate and socialize their children for success. Each chapter ends with family activities that will increase character development, cultural competence and critical thinking skills.

Black History Power Pak!
By Dr. Chike Akua

The Black History Power Pak is a collection of 7 books by Dr. Chike Akua. It is a wonderful way to supplement your current lessons. Use to it show your students the beauty of African and African American culture and contributions. Increase and improve reading comprehension, cultural awareness, and character development.

XIIIIXIIIIXIIIIXIII   Chike Akua, Ph.D.   **XIIIIXIIIIXIIIIXIII**

Reading Revolution: Reconnecting the Roots
By Dr. Chike Akua & Tavares Stephens

A collection of 90 reading selections about African and African American people of extraordinary accomplishment. Use *Reading Revolution* to improve reading comprehension and cultural consciousness at the same time:
- Standardized test format with multiple choice questions
- Topic, main idea, supporting details and sequencing
- Vocabulary development and context clues
- Making inferences and drawing conclusions

"Chike Akua and Tavares Stephens combine excellent teaching skills, deep knowledge of African history and culture, and, as Master Teachers, a real grasp of students' interests and thinking. Reading Revolution is an outstanding product of this mixture, and hence a rare value for schools."
  Asa G. Hilliard III-Nana Baffour Amankwatia II, Ed.D.
  Fuller E. Calloway Professor of Urban Education
  Georgia State University

"At a time when teachers across the nation are struggling to find the delicate balance between curricular standards and meaningful content that students will readily identify with, Mr. Akua and Mr. Stephens have definitely hit the mark with Reading Revolution."
  Vonzia Phillips, Ph.D., Director of Premiere Middle Schools
  Dekalb County School District
  Atlanta, GA

Chike Akua and Tavares Stephens have crafted a masterful publication which makes reading, vocabulary building and comprehension memorable learning experiences."
  Anthony T. Browder, Author
  Nile Valley Contributions to Civilization

XIIIIXIIIIXIIIIXIII Chike Akua, Ph.D. **XIIIIXIIIIXIIIIXIII**

A Treasure Within: Stories of Remembrance & Rediscovery
By Dr. Chike Akua

"What would it be like to meet an ancient African Ancestor? Marcus, Imani, and Daniel are about to find out! *A Treasure Within* is a book of three short stories in which young people have encounters with ancient African ancestors to learn about traditional African morals, values, history, and culture.

"A Treasure Within *is the book that many of us have been waiting for. The deep thinking of Ancient Africa is grasped and communicated clearly through these three powerful stories. Families, counselors, teachers, students, and the community, in general, can relate directly to these stories...I am thankful for this outstanding contribution to our mental and spiritual liberation. Our Ancestors are pleased. Amun is satisfied."*

    Asa G. Hilliard III – Nana Baffour Amankwatia II, Ed.D.
    Fuller E. Calloway Professor of Urban Education
    Georgia State University

"Chike Akua, a Master Teacher, engages the reader with three compelling stories. His mastery of the written word intertwined with historical facts and cultural revelations invites the reader to be totally immersed. Readers of all ages will enjoy this literary rites of passage."
    Phyllis Daniel, Principal
    Stephenson Middle School
    Stone Mountain, GA

A Treasure Within: Parent/Teacher Resource Guide

This book is a complete companion curriculum to *A Treasure Within: Stories of Remembrance & Rediscovery*. It includes a wide range of activities to reinforce content objectives and develop character, cultural awareness, and commitment.

"...for teachers and parents who believe that classrooms and homes are places where the child's spirit is cultivated and soars, A Treasure Within: Stories of Remembrance & Rediscovery *and the accompanying* Parent/Teacher Resource Guide *provides a path – a path to knowledge and understanding."*
    Leslie T. Fenwick, Ph.D.
    Professor Of Educational Policy, Clark Atlanta University
    Visiting Scholar, Harvard School of Education

"A Treasure Within is a remarkable collection of stories with a broad appeal to all youth. The stories instruct, develop moral character, and entertain at the same time. The accompanying Parent/Teacher Resource Guide *is a great and useful addition to this wonderful collection."*
    Dr. William Hammond, Reading Instruction Coordinator
    Dekalb County School District
    Atlanta, Georgia

A Kwanzaa Awakening: Lessons for the Community

A Kwanzaa Awakening is a resource with activities for everyone. Parents, educators, and clergy will find activities for children K-12 and beyond. It includes:
- A Brief History of Kwanzaa
- Kwanzaa Classroom Activities (grades 6-12)
- Lessons for the Little Ones (K-5)
- A 3-act Play
- Worksheets and Puzzles
- Quiz and Test
- Coloring Activities
- Writing Activities
- Poetry
- Reading Comprehension Selections
- Kwanzaa in Christ: How to Celebrate Kwanzaa in the Church
- Kwanzaa and the Qu'ran: Islamic Expressions of the Seven Principles
- Glossary

"Through this book, Akua provides ways for us to value the lives of our children and ways to teach them who they are as children with a rich African heritage. This book...challenges us to train our children in ways that will affirm our past and secure our future."

James C. Anyike, M.Div.
Author, *African American Holidays*

XIIIIXIIIIXIIIIXIII Chike Akua, Ph.D. **XIIIIXIIIIXIIIIXIII**

Words of Power, Volume 1: Ancient Insights and Modern Messages for Parents, Teachers & Students   By Chike Akua

This book contains almost 200 quotes and proverbs from African people and powerful people all over the world. Additionally it contains fill-in worksheets so that students can engage in a words of wisdom scavenger hunt.

Share the mother wit and wisdom that many of our children today are missing as you examine and interpret figurative language, simile and metaphor.

Words of Power, Volume 2: Centering Ourselves for Excellence   By Chike Akua

In the compelling follow-up to Volume 1, this book contains almost 250 quotes and proverbs from African people and powerful people all over the world. Additionally it contains fill-in worksheets so that students can engage in a words of wisdom scavenger hunt.

This book helps student understand literal and figurative language as they receive the much needed mother wit and wisdom of Elders and Ancestors.

Sexceptional: The Ultimate and Essential Teen Guide to Abstinence

By Chike Akua

Sexceptional is an adjective that describes "one who is willing to undertake the discipline, devotion, and determination to abstain from sexual activity until marriage." It takes an exceptional person because there are many weapons of mass distraction and weapons of mass deception. We hear a lot about safe sex, but abstinence is, hands down, the safest alternative. But when abstinence is mentioned, oftentimes young people are not given the tools to make abstinence work. This book is a tool box of insights and strategies.

What Does It Mean To Be Black? DVD (Recorded LIVE!) By Chike Akua

Chike Akua asks the quintessential question that requires a radical redefinition of Blackness. This dynamic and revealing DVD give students an understanding of Africa's contributions to reading and writing, language and literature, science and technology, math and medicine, and so much more! A picture is worth a thousand words and this DVD visually documents African excellence, achievement, and ingenuity—ancient and modern.

XIIIIXIIIIXIIIIXIII   Chike Akua, Ph.D.   **XIIIIXIIIIXIIIIXIII**

Black History Poster Pak!
By Chike Akua
*Purchase the whole Pak for your school and get one <u>FREE</u>!

These beautiful, full-size, color posters on the following pages are both inspirational and instructional. They are a wonderful addition to any classroom, office or living room. Developed and designed by award-winning educator and author, Dr. Chike Akua, these posters are a rich resource for creating a culture of excellence and achievement in your classroom or school.

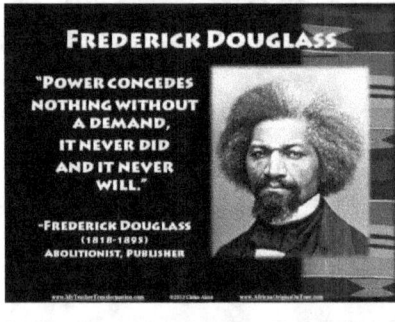

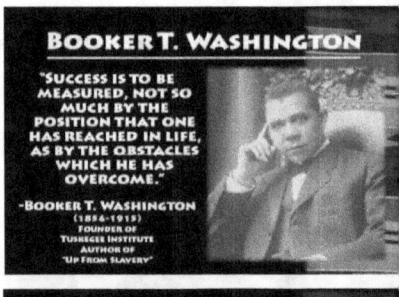
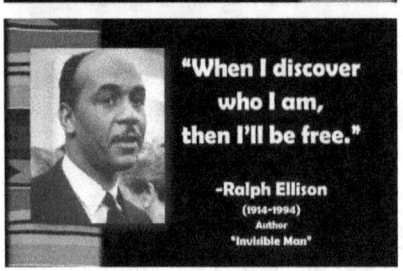
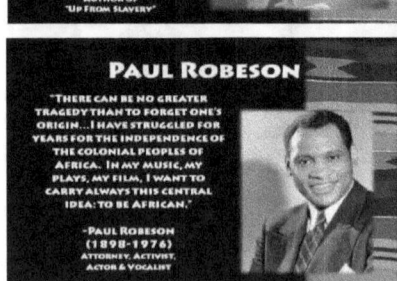

XIIIIXIIIIXIIIIXIII   Chike Akua, Ph.D.   XIIIIXIIIIXIIIIXIII

Honoring Our Ancestral Obligations

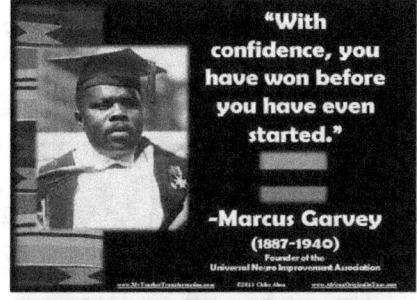
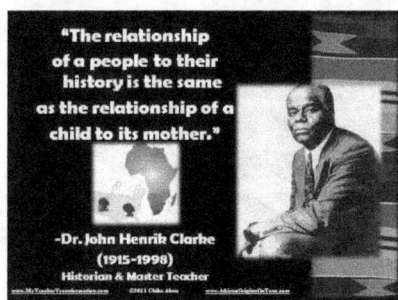

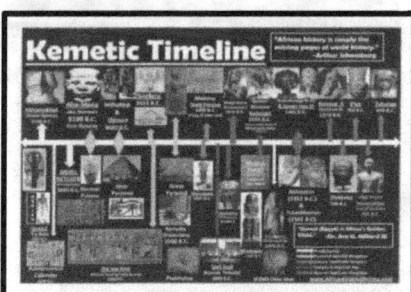
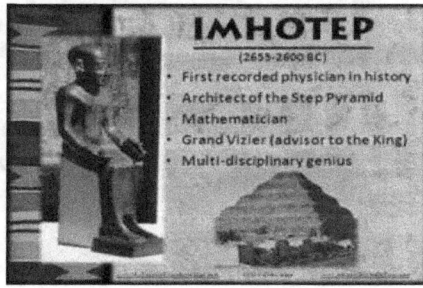

XIIIIXIIIIXIIIIXIII   Chike Akua, Ph.D.   XIIIIXIIIIXIIIIXIII

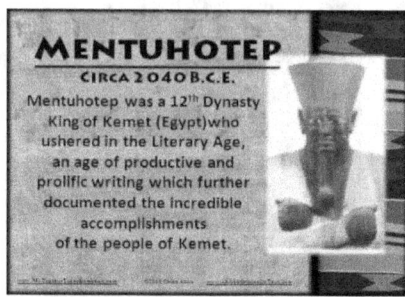
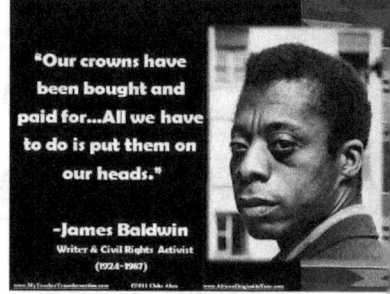

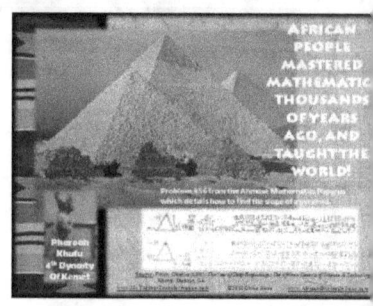

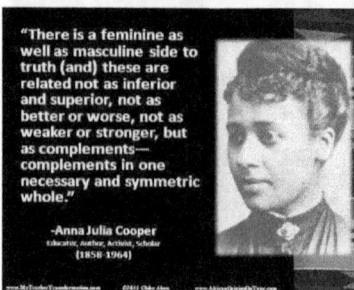

Honoring Our Ancestral Obligations

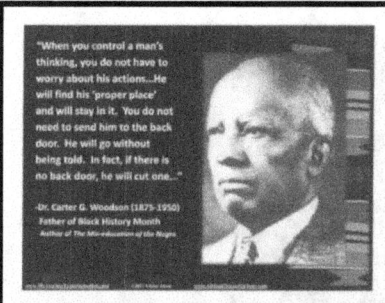
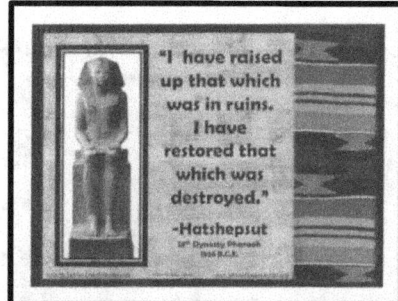

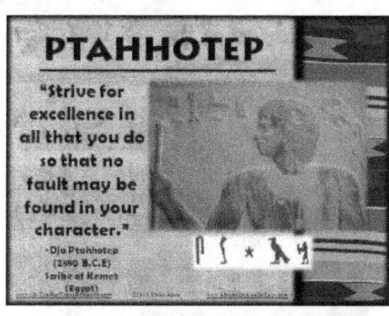
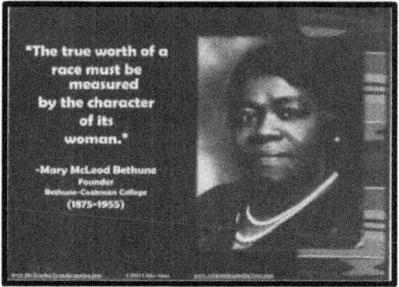
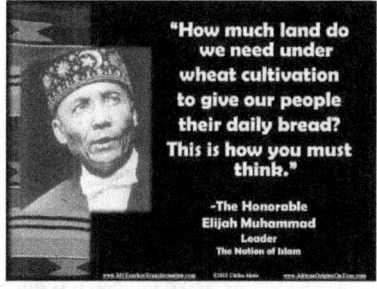

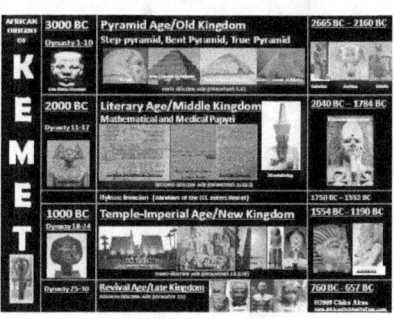

XIIIIXIIIIXIIIIXIII   Chike Akua, Ph.D.   XIIIIXIIIIXIIIIXIII

Honoring Our Ancestral Obligations

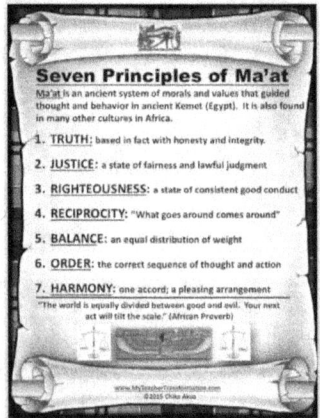

Order books, posters, and DVDs at
www.DrAkua.net

Chike Akua, Ph.D.

www.ingramcontent.com/pod-product-compliance
Lightning Source LLC
Chambersburg PA
CBHW071922290426
44110CB00013B/1448